Boc

MW01109292

Voices
FROM THE FIELD

CONVERSATIONS WITH OUR GLOBAL FAMILY

Executive Editor
T.J. MacLeslie

peregrini press

Llantwit Major, Wales
2018

Voices from the Field: Conversations with Our Global Family

Illustrations by Anna Newcomb
Email: annamakinzie@googlemail.com

For inquiries related to this book please contact us.
Email: info@peregrinipress.com
Tel: +44-(0)7597-170650

FOR THOSE WHO HAVE GONE BEFORE US
AND THOSE WHO WILL COME AFTER

"WE HAVE TWO EARS AND ONE TONGUE
SO THAT WE WOULD LISTEN MORE AND TALK LESS"

DIOGENES
(412 BC)

TABLE OF CONTENTS

FOREWORD

It has been a great honour to read this blessed and rich endeavour that brings us all in front of the honest words of precious indigenous men and women of God. These local believers have made themselves vulnerable while boldly telling the truth that we sometimes do not want to hear.

If the heart of every problem is the problem of the heart, then we may need to examine our hearts in God's presence as we read through this unique book.

As a former missionary to the country of Sudan and currently a fellow worker in the field of training future cross-cultural workers, I do admit that I have made my own mistakes in the mission field. I the process I have discovered that we learn more from our mistakes (if we are sincere and honest) than from our achievements.

Two quotes from this book that you are about to read are eye opening for us all:

> *"I think they (foreigners) have good understanding on the superficial things but don't have a good understanding of our deeper things..."*

> *"Relationships are very important to us. So when we arrange to see a foreigner and they cancel, it makes us feel very bad because we don't do this. Our busyness doesn't take place of our relationships."*

Every culture has its own defects as a result of the fallen world we live in, no one is perfect. This book reminds us of our Master, who gave time to every individual who met and needed Him; Jesus did not consider interruptions as hurdles but opportunities. The One who commissioned us: "As the Father has sent me, even so I am sending you", (John 20:21) is still calling you and I to fix our eyes firmly on Him and to humbly learn how to present Him wisely.

My prayers go with this work, may the Lord use it powerfully for His glory. I encourage each new worker to spend enough time here to ponder the values engraved in each page of these "voices" from a diversity of many lands. Even after we spend some years in the field, you and I continue to be students till the end. Read it carefully and pass copies to your team(s).

"Voices" can be God's voice to you as you continue the journey to advance the gospel of our Lord. (Phil. 1:12)

Many thanks to our brother TJ MacLeslie who is giving us another gift after the earlier "Forged" which has enriched many lives.

Mafdy Armanious
DMIN, Trinity Evangelical Divinity School
Cairo, Egypt, 2018

PREFACE

This book was birthed by a passing comment from my friend, Dr. Lazarus Phiri. He was speaking on another topic, but remarked on the dearth of African voices in Christian conversations even though the African church makes up a very large proportion of the global church. His comment stirred something in me. I started praying about how to help us, the global church, to hear these oft neglected voices.

Over time, God birthed in me a passion for this endeavour, and I launched the project that would become this book. I really did not think it would be this difficult. I started this project more than three years ago, initially contacting nearly 200 missionaries around the world, asking them to interview local brothers and sisters. The previous volume in this series took less than a year from start to finish. I anticipated that this one would be similar. I could not have been more mistaken.

The first barrier I hit was the hesitance of my colleagues on the mission field to hear what their local friends might want to say. Several responded that they were afraid of what local church leaders would say about them. Some were confident that they knew exactly what they would say and therefore did not want to ask. Still others were unwilling to ask questions without knowing what the outcome would be. They sought some sort of guarantee about the perspectives that would be presented in the book; guarantees I was not willing or able to give.

Surely we can't decide what our brothers and sisters would be allowed to say, or sit in judgement on what we would publish, before we even had listened to them. In the end, although I was disappointed by these responses, I recognised my own fear in the fear of my friends. I, too, have been unwilling to listen or afraid to ask far too often in my life. Over time, I was pleased to find that some expatriate missionaries were willing to overcome their fears and confront their own biases. The submissions began to trickle in, but very slowly.

The second barrier I encountered surprised me more and was, perhaps, even more sorrowful. Many of my friends and mission colleagues are from the majority, non-Western world (for we, "Western" Christians, now represent less than half of global Christians). I asked them to contribute their voices, and to interview Christians and church leaders they knew. Virtually none of them responded. As time passed, and I wrote repeatedly, or talked with them when our paths crossed at various events or conferences, I began to hear various riffs on this refrain, "I didn't think you really wanted to hear from us. Many times we are invited to the table but no one really wants to listen to us. We are invited to sit at the table, but not really invited to speak. I (We) just assumed you didn't really want to hear from us." This broke my heart.

It is hard for me to imagine the privilege that has been afforded to me. Because of my skin colour, my gender, my education, and the point at which we find ourselves as a global society, I simply and profoundly believe that my voices is valid, desired even. It is nearly impossible for me to understand the courage necessary for my brothers and sisters to raise their voices and to offer their honest perspective. Eventually, some found their courage and offered their voices.

You hold a treasure in your hands today. You will likely never have the opportunity to meet the people in this volume. Each captured voice is a real person, living in some corner of the world. Each one offers their unique perspective and opportunity for growth and change. I pray we will listen. More than that, I pray this book will help us all find more courage to ask, to listen, and to converse with each other.

My wife is fond of saying that a true conversation is when both people come into it willing to be changed. We seem to be losing the art of conversation. We often only listen to those with whom we already agree. Or, even worse, love the sound of our own voices so much that we never really listen to anyone else. In this book, I expect, you will find unfamiliar voices, perhaps you will be offended or perplexed. I know I have been. But these are the honest voices of our family and they should be, must be, heard. We must be willing to be changed.

True conversations take place along the way. As we are going, we find ourselves seated next to someone on a bus or a plane, for those few minutes we share a leg of the journey of our lives. These days, we (particularly in the West) are caught up in our screens and distracted and we miss the opportunities for real conversation along the way. Don't miss this opportunity to converse with strangers made in the image of God.

One note about these voices – We have made every effort to edit the submissions very lightly, if at all. While this may make the book a little harder to read, we hope it will help to retain the authentic voices and thoughts of our global family. Read carefully and listen well, try to catch the accent and intonation not just the words on the page. As you read, be thinking about how local people in your context might answer these questions. Consider picking a few questions and approaching church leaders and trusted friends to hear their experience and seek their feedback and input. You will probably hear perspectives you have not heard before and learn to better see the world through their eyes.

Today, I invite you to imagine yourself walking the hot, dusty road of life. As you go, you find yourself walking alongside a stranger. Up ahead you see a tree and some welcome shade. I invite you to sit down under the tree with each of these people in turn and listen to their voices. I suspect you will be changed when you do. I know I have been.

Thaddaeus Joseph MacLeslie
Llantwit Major, Wales 2018

SODNOM – MONGOLIA

Her eyes dance with enthusiasm and her bright smile touches everyone she meets. Sodnom, a petite, attractive lady in her early sixties, is a smartly-dressed and well-

> They had tried to understand our culture and be sensitive to God.

educated Mongolian. But it's not her intellect or her neatness that draws people. No, it's her passionate love for Jesus.

"Sodnom egch, can you tell me how the Lord has worked in your life and how I might grow in my understanding of your culture and the workings of God?"

"Of course," she replied. "But let me begin by saying that the Lord was working in my life long before I ever met a Christian missionary or heard the gospel."

I settled comfortably into the chair in her church office. Sodnom has been a Christian for more than twenty years. She is currently a church elder and, together with a team of five Mongolians, is preparing to work on a new translation of the Bible.

"From the age of one," she said thoughtfully, "I lived with my grandparents. They were herders and lived in the real countryside away from other towns and villages in a ger. When I was five years old, my grandfather (who was also a Buddhist lama) told me about the one big God who lived in the sky. He told me that God could see me all the time. He saw when I did good things which pleased Him, and He saw when I did bad things that He didn't like.

"His words," she said slowly, "were like a seed in my young heart; they lodged deeply and something in me knew they were true."

Sodnom grew up during the Russian Communism era, a time when the state taught that there were no gods, no spirits - good or evil - and no religion.

"At the age of eight," she continued, "I returned to my parents in the village as I needed to start school. There the teachers taught us that there was no God. With my head I accepted and believed this teaching, as they told us these facts were scientifically correct. My head became filled with knowledge, and outwardly at least, I looked the same as everyone else; but in my heart I felt differently. And I wondered where the God my grandfather had told me about was.

"I had so many questions but no one could answer them, as we were only permitted to speak about things which were purportedly proven. We were encouraged to study hard to gain knowledge and become good, competent people.

"I became a school teacher and when I taught the children, I simply regurgitated what I had been taught. I told them there was no spiritual world — that there was no God. I told them man was the highest creature in this world and that by his own strength he could do anything," she smiled. "On reflection, I was saying that man was God."

Pausing for a moment she smoothed her skirt. "I come from a very different world to you," she said, "and this is something missionaries need to understand."

I nodded, "Your world is a rich world full of tradition and culture. Please help me understand that world."

She continued, "Then in my mid-twenties my grandfather died. My grandmother died when I was young, and although that was sad time, I didn't feel her death like I felt my grandfather's. He was a special part of my life; I loved him deeply, but he was also the unspoken anchor holding me to the banished world of his big God. I knew he spoke to God on my behalf. With him gone I felt fearful and wondered what would become of me and my children, for by then I was married with my own family.

"I had no answers other than I knew I needed a person like my grandfather who would connect with God on my behalf, because I believed I couldn't. Now I understand that I was searching for the true God; but I had to come to see that there was no peace or life in Buddhism."

"Didn't Communism ban religious beliefs?" I asked.

"It did, but behind closed ger doors we continued our Buddhist and Shamanistic practices."

"Do you think foreign missionaries understood this?"

"No," she replied quickly. "Missionaries are impatient and try to force the gospel on us without knowing the history and context of our lives."

"I am sorry," I said. "Please forgive us for our impatience."

"Missionaries must understand the journey we have to make in order to truly embrace the gospel."

"You are right; I want to understand more clearly," I said, motioning for Sodnom to continue with her story.

She smiled, "Therefore, I went to Buddhist lamas and shamans — in fact I went to anyone who I thought might give me guidance and protection.

"But my husband, Enkee, was different to me. He was a pure Communist thinker. He truly didn't believe in the existence of the spiritual world. He believed only in man, and that with education and knowledge he could achieve anything. In the quietness of our home he began teasing me. He wasn't angry — he just ridiculed me. I wasn't happy but I kept going to the lamas anyway."

By the early 1990s Russian communism had disintegrated and Mongolia began the transition towards a democracy. For the first time in seventy years the country opened its doors to the west; and missionaries, who had been waiting for such an opening, flooded in sharing the good news of the gospel as they came. The whole church then numbered less than four or five believers but quickly burgeoned as young people, hungry for spiritual reality, pounced on the gospel.

"In 1993 we met an American couple called Jon and Vonnie," said Sodnom, "and I became Vonnie's, Mongolian language teacher. Once we took them to visit the province where Enkee and I had grown up. We travelled by train and the wife, I remember, started talking to me about Jesus. I told her, 'Of course Jesus is your God — you westerners. Many people still think the same.

"But our god is different, we are Mongolians and we believe in Buddha. Imagine we are all climbing up a mountain from different sides, I said…Buddhists, Christians and Muslims. We come by different ways but we all reach the same summit, so I don't need your Jesus.

"Wisely they didn't say anything, but prayed." Sodnom stopped and raised her finger. "I think this is a very important lesson for missionaries to learn. Remember that you are guests in our country and even though you disagree with us, please do not ridicule us or judge us for our beliefs. You need to respect our beliefs and traditions.

"Let me repeat that Jon and Vonnie didn't force the gospel on us, but I'm sure they were praying for us. They did show us 'The Jesus Film' and Enkee and I thought, 'They are good people, but deeply misguided in their belief that their dead, so-called saviour could rise from the dead.'

"By then we were teaching Mongolian to a number of missionaries and we were becoming friends with these people. As a part of their language lessons they asked us to help them read and understand the newly-published Mongolian New Testament. Of course, wanting to help my students do well, I readily agreed to this new idea; and in preparation for the lessons, I started reading the Bible myself. I thought, 'Wow, what great lessons — this book is right and truthful.' I happily embraced the teaching but I didn't want the religion.

"Then some of our students invited us to church. Again I felt comfortable going with them. They were kind and thoughtful and we knew that they cared for us; these odd foreigners were becoming our friends. I took one of my daughters, Eree, with me. I told her, 'Listen to the teaching but don't accept the religion.' Of course, she was young and impressionable and within two months she'd become a Christian. Enkee did not like that and told her to stop being a Christian, but she didn't. She kept reading her Bible and going to church.

"Determined to prove Eree wrong, Enkee started reading the New Testament and quickly found portions that made him angry. He wanted to know why the church was teaching our daughter such error. We contacted a young Korean pastor who promised to come to our home and give us answers, but he was too busy; so my husband asked an American couple, who were our students, to explain these wrong teachings to us.

"This older couple said that they could not answer Enkee's questions directly, but rather wisely told us if we wanted to find the right answers to our questions then we needed to study the Bible from the beginning to the end. They asked us if we wanted to do that and we said yes — thinking that way we'd easily expose our daughter's errors.

"We began meeting in September 1994," she said with a sigh. "We met twice a week but our studies seemed tediously slow as our American friends only spoke a little Mongolian and I only knew a little English, although Enkee knew Russian well and had a Russian Bible. I had an English children's Bible, as the Old Testament had not been published then. Yet despite our slow progress the Holy Spirit was working.

"This older couple never told us what to believe; rather they prayed, asking God's Word to speak into our lives in a way that we could understand.

"Two months after we started, we were reading through Psalm 139. 'I praise you for I am fearfully and wonderfully made,' it says. Suddenly those amazing words stuck a chord in my heart and I realised — this is the God I have been searching for, this is the God my grandfather told me about. I was forty one years old and I'd been searching for Him for more than thirty years.

"Tears streamed down my face, '...for you formed my inward parts...' I'd heard a lot about Jesus but this was the first time His Word deeply touched my heart, and for the first time I came face to face with my sin. You see, I had aborted children that God had given me and at that moment I saw my sin as God saw it; and completely broken, I wept in repentance.

"I wondered what Enkee would be thinking about my tears; but glancing at him I saw that he was weeping too, and at the same time we both said, 'Amazing.'

"Our American friends had taken us to God's Word and allowed it to speak to our lives. They had tried to understand our culture and be sensitive to God. Never once did they focus on their experiences of God and try to force them on to us; rather, they allowed God to speak to us in a way that connected to us our hearts.

"From that moment we didn't look back. We believed wholeheartedly. We went to church; but not only that, we knew we must tell people about Jesus. We didn't know much but we told people what we knew, and our family and friends started coming to know the Lord. God did many amazing, wonderful things; but our lives were also touched by tragedy.

"Eree, our daughter, who came to know the Lord first, drowned in England; and then Enkee died from liver cancer. Mongolians believe adherence to, and respect of, the Buddhist and Shamanist ways will keep the spirits happy and give us a good life. When people saw us suffering, they naturally assumed we were bad people.

"But our missionary friends kept re-orientating us to God and His Word alone. They made no judgement, but again let the Word of God speak into our lives. Their respect enabled us to find God in the midst of sorrow and allow Him to work out His purposes. Enkee's funeral was an incredible testimony to the goodness of God that touched people's lives and brought some back to Him."

Her face is alight with praise for God as she talks, and then with a note of seriousness she adds, "Sometimes I hear people whisper behind my back that I've experienced such suffering because I accepted a foreign religion. But I tell them everyone experiences sorrow in life. And I know it's in the middle of suffering that God draws closer to me and becomes more real. Jesus takes my suffering and gives it shape and brings meaning through it into my life; because without Him there truly would be no hope."

She grabs my hand. "God used missionaries to help us see the realities of the gospel. He sent godly, mature people who came alongside us and never their forced religion on us. They walked with us and we learned together. It is wonderful when missionaries go overseas, but over the years we have seen some people come and not be sensitive to the voices of the people around them. They have tried to force their gospel on us and it doesn't fit. I want to say to new missionaries, 'Realise that you will be living in a new world. Seek to understand this world and the people you work with. Be sensitive to God and His leading; be sensitive to your new environment and be prepared to change.'"

ANDRES – MEXICO

What would you want someone new coming into your area to know?

That even if their nations are richer or more powerful, their home culture and their form of Christianity is not the only one around, nor the best. They will need to not only learn a

> *I pray you will be able to not only function in my culture, but to enjoy it, be enriched, and perhaps even be changed by it for the better.*

language but also a whole different cultural lifestyle. They will need to adapt to and adopt in many ways. They should expect to come as learners before trying to be workers or teachers.

If missionaries were going to come to your town, what would you want them to know before arriving?

I believe it would be very useful for them to learn about my country's history and culture, and also to get in touch with the local believers or other missionaries. They should get to know the work the locals are doing before trying to "save" my community with their particular "mission." It would be very important for them to consider partnering in a respectful way with existing believers instead of going it on their own.

It would be good for them to know beforehand what the risks and discomforts are of living and working here compared to what their home countries are like, so they will know what to expect.

It would also be very important for them to get some training in worldview and working cross-culturally (3D Gospel, etc.) and in the realities of spiritual warfare.

What do you think is the most important thing for a foreigner to understand about your culture/people?

That we value relationships above work and achievements and that time is very fluid and not strict. That we enjoy having good times together and that it might be more productive to have fun together than to achieve much. That it's important to care for people's honor and feelings and avoid situations of shame. That there is a long and complicated relationship between my culture and Western countries that sets a background for people from those cultures that they might not be aware of.

How would you like to see new people relate to/partner with your church?

To relate with a humble and learning attitude, willing to serve in whatever need they're invited to help with, even if it doesn't imply leadership. To be careful not to bring so many resources that they create dependency or a belittling situation for leaders. To make and enjoy relationships and learn to enjoy a different worship style. In general I would like to see them enjoy my church.

If you could speak to a group of young missionaries being trained, what would you say to them?

Although it will be a tremendous challenge, I pray you will be able to not only function in my culture, but to enjoy it, be enriched, and perhaps even be changed by it for the better. I pray you not only come to "get the mission done" but to become, as much as possible, one of us.

PAUL – MALI

Where were you born, your family and your education?

Sinaly Koné, born in Macina, in a Bambara, Muslim, and polygamous family. I went to French and Koranic school. I went to school in Macina.

> *I have not known any living missionary here, who is contributing in any church, or putting his evangelistic materials to the benefit of the common ministry.*

Are you employed and if so, what are you doing now?

I am a pastor and missionary on Pioneers' account.

How did you meet Jesus? Share your story briefly.

I met Jesus Christ through a Ghanaian missionary called Dr. Solomon Aryeetey. After attending many of his evangelistic programs, and watching the movie Jesus and other films, I finally understood God's love and compassion through the life of Christ Jesus, his suffering and his dead on the cross in our place. There I decided to stop following Islam, the religion of my parents, and to be a disciple of the Saviour Jesus Christ, who did everything to give his life to redeem me.

What kind of church do you attend? - Tell a typical Sunday service

Currently, I attend a native church in Mali, precisely in Segou city, the fourth administrative region of the country. I take part fully in the various services of Sunday worship. As a pastor, I preach in many churches, as part of the mobilization for the mission in Mali.

Do you have a relationship or connection with missionaries living in your city / town?

Yes I have relations with several missionaries living in Mali: Segou, Bamoko, Kayes, Tenenkou...

How do you feel about their involvement in churches?

In my opinion, they are not engaged as full members in local churches. Instead of adding their effort to that of the church, they prefer to work solo. I have not known any living missionary here, who is contributing in any church, or putting his evangelistic materials to the benefit of the common ministry.

What are some of the common cultural mistakes or misunderstandings foreigners make in your country?

Some of the errors committed by these missionaries are:

They always stand on the margins of the community where they live, even Christian.

Often in the context of contextualization, they go so far as to change their name and surname. This creates problems because the people think they are hiding their real names. People do not take it seriously, because hiding one's true identity creates trust issues.

At the end of their stay here, on their way home they sell all their and this gives the impression that they love money much more than the gospel they came to announce. I think they had to help the needy with these clothes and materials already used, to support their messages with acts of compassion. Instead of selling the things the church needs to continue the ministry, they could leave them to brothers who need them for the efficiency of their ministry.

What are some of the areas of conflict that you observe among the foreign community?

1. Not respecting the tradition and culture of others

2. Failure to take into account the ideas and suggestions of the host community
3. Failure to take into account the real needs of communities

Where do you feel this arises from?
1. These conflicts come from the superiority complex of Westerners relative to Africans.
2. The non-recognition of African values.
3. Inequality in treatment and recognition of merit.

What do you feel about their levels of understanding of your culture and context?

Many of our missionary brothers think that they have to change the way of thinking and doing of Africans. For this reason they do not think they have to look for us or listen to us, but they want us to listen to them and that we become like them.

AHMED AND LOUBNA – MOROCCO

My dream is to see the Moroccan church grow and become strong, and I believe this is possible. There are scattered believers in different parts of the country. They feel very much alone because they are not in

> *Local believers know how their own people think and can discern their true motivation, something which foreigners often miss.*

fellowship with other believers. I envision visiting and spending time with those in cities nearby while another like-minded brother does the same thing with believers near to the city where he lives. We will find out why a certain believer is not in fellowship with others, introduce him to believers in the area and then teach and encourage them in their faith. This can take the form of a monthly visit or a 3-day Bible study or a discipleship camp. Once this is ongoing, isolated believers will no longer struggle alone and may likewise catch the vision of a Moroccan church that can withstand challenges and opposition.

The church in Morocco was very much shaken when foreigners were expelled in 2010. Different groups used to gather together once a month to know how each was doing and what activities each group was engaged in. But after that event, everything came to a grinding halt. The number of believers significantly dwindled. Even those who attended the expatriate church disappeared. Needless to say, believers were afraid. There were no strong disciples.

However, in the last two years the church has bounced back and grown a bit. There are churches in quite a few cities (Tangier, Casa,

Agadir, and Marrakesh) and the relationship between churches is good. I talk with and see some of them from time to time.

I remember a time when there used to be 35 groups meeting in different places. The question is, "Where are they now?" One of the reasons they disappeared was because there were no teachers.

This is where foreigners can come in. They can sometimes come to the church to teach the Word of God. They can do discipleship training or Bible studies in the homes. This way believers can once again see each other as brothers and once equipped, can also teach others. In this regard there is no difference between a foreigner and a Moroccan, since both of them are servants of God. The Lord is all. He is the head of the church. There is no other.

Foreigners who are planning to come here should bear in mind several things:

They should pray and ask God what He wants them to do. When they follow the will of God, they will succeed; otherwise, they will accomplish nothing.

They should meet with the leaders of the church and find out what they need. Doing so will give them insight into the condition of the church and what they can do to help the church grow.

They should know the Word of God and evaluate the correctness of what is being taught in the church so believers can live according to Scriptures.

They need to be wise and not easily taken in by locals' professions of faith. I say that because I am actually afraid that here the likes of Judas Iscariot are present in the church. You see, another reason why the church "disappeared" was though some who professed to believe were meeting with the foreigner, they did not really embrace the latter's faith. For them, Jesus was still the "god of the foreigner." When the foreigner left, those so-called believers turned away from the faith.

In the past, foreigners would meet with a local person outside of the church and study the Word with him. However, they would not bring him to the church. This is not ideal. Local believers know how their own people think and can discern their true motivation, something which foreigners often miss. Sometimes they seem too eager to believe what they hear. Hence, it is advisable that a foreigner takes a believer when he meets with a local.

It is imperative that they share the Word of God and from it show the truth about the Lord Jesus Christ. But before they do, they must first establish relationship with people and determine what kind of relationship it will be. The kind of relationship one has with the local person will determine when he can share the Gospel with the latter.

They should learn the language as well as the culture of the place they are going to. There are different people groups and each has a language and culture of its own. Learning both will undoubtedly help them relate with people.

Nowadays, people do not have problems with someone being of another faith, with someone being a Christian. I believe the real problem now is "Daeesh" (ISIS). However, should persecution like the one in 2010 happen again, foreign workers can be of assistance by helping us enlist the aid of a lawyer.

The fulfilment of the vision I have is not going to come easy. For instance, I have asked some people to come back, but thus far I have not received a response. However, I am not discouraged. I believe we should pray for them so the Lord will bring them back to the fold. Only He can bring a person, when that person is ready. Therefore, we must pray so He will do something that will glorify His name.

I can confidently say that because it was the Lord Himself who drew me to Him when He deemed me ready. It was 1987; I was young and I was looking for the truth. To find it, I enrolled in correspondence courses and compared the Injil with the Qur'an.

Then one day I had a dream. The Lord Jesus gave me a sign. There was the sea and images of war. God was in the middle, with an angel to His right and another to His left. Jesus came near me and declared, "I am the way, the truth, and the life. Come!" And He left.

I had to make a decision that day and I did. I accepted Jesus. That was in 1990. I was twenty-six years old. From 1999 till about three years ago, I have had dreams of the Lord around twenty-six times. The last time I dreamed of Him, He gave me water to drink. It was very good; I drank and drank. He gave me an apple and I ate it. Then He left.

I was blessed to have met with many people after I became a believer. However, my wife was not a believer when we got married. She often says that it was because she could not read much and did not know. However, I believed it was because she was not yet ready and the Lord knew. She did come to know the way of the Lord. Then, the miracle of being granted a son in answer to prayers further strengthened her faith.

So yes, the fulfilment of the vision will not come easy. Neither will its implementation; it will need the help of other believers in terms of logistics and financial contribution. No one can do a task like this alone. But it can be done when we work together. God will bless our efforts.

If I have the chance to speak to those who are thinking of coming here, I would tell them two more things in addition to what I have already said. First, come with wisdom and be as peaceful as doves. Second, strengthen the relationship between us. By these, their time will be fruitful.

PRIYA – INDIA

We sit cross legged on the bed, in Priya's small 2-room apartment that she shares with her husband and daughter. The room is dim as the curtains are closed against the heat of the day, giving us little relief. I have only known Priya for a few years but she has become very dear to me and very much my

> *The biggest thing I have seen is that foreign couples, when they come into church and sit down together and are hugging during the preaching, it is distracting and you end up looking at them and not listening to the sermon.*

Indian family. She is a Bengali in her 50s and has such peace, joy and a love of others that do not betray the vast difficulties that she has experienced throughout her life.

Tell me your story: where you were born, about your family and upbringing etc.

I was born in Kolkata. I was the 3rd of 6 children. I had 2 older and 1 younger brothers and 2 younger sisters. We were a Hindu family. We lived in small house with 4 rooms, but 2 of those rooms were rented out. The house was mostly made of concrete but it had 1 mud wall and tin roof. We were a poor family and life was very hard. It was like this…often we would go to school having not eaten, we didn't have school books, and we relied on people to give us free pens to use at school. Basically my childhood was a real struggle.

Where did you go to school?

I went to a Bengali medium school. I finished school and after went to a Bengali college to study pure arts. However, I also had to work. I would work before school delivering milk to people to earn a few pennies. I would also give tuition to younger children and I would help in various ways in the neighbourhood.

Are you employed and if so what are you doing now?

Yes, I am a Bengali translator. I work with foreigners who come into town and translate for them.

My husband used to live in the village but he had family living in the house next door to us. So one time he came to Kolkata for some work. He had a 4 year-old niece who also came with him, along with his mother. I used to love children, so through that niece I would go to their house and in that way I met my husband. I and started chatting with him and we fell in love with each other.

I asked if her family were happy with the match, because at that time love match was not allowed. She answered, "Firstly, my family was poor and his was fairly rich and the family well-known. So my family were scared. At first his family were not happy but after they got to know me it was ok."

How did you meet Jesus? Share your testimony briefly with me.

After my marriage I stayed at home. One day my neighbour came to my house; it was a Hindu festival that day. I had offered some sweets to the goddess Lakshmi, whose festival it was, and so when my neighbour came to visit I gave her some of the sweets I had offered to Lakshmi. But my neighbour said she could not take it. I thought a lot about what she was saying and when I asked her why she couldn't take it, she said it would be a big sin. So she would not agree to take it and said that if I give it forcefully I would be sinning. So I didn't give it to her, but when she left I talked with my husband about what she had said. I thought on this and one day visited my neighbour and slowly came to know about Jesus. That first day I went to my neighbour's house was the first day in my life that I felt peace. I had had so much trouble in my life. From my childhood time life had been hard, so that first day I heard about Jesus was the first day I felt peace.

I asked how long it took from the first time she heard about Jesus to believing in Him. Her answer: It took 6 months to fully believe in Him. I felt His peace, I knew He was with me, but I was still worshiping the Hindu gods as well. It took 3 years to only worship Him. My husband was not happy I had become a Christian; he would torture me, we had many arguments and he said we would separate. But after 4-5 years he also became a Christian.

What sort of church do you attend? – tell me about a typical Sunday service.

I go to a very good church. They are my family, my well-wishers, they guide me, and they are everything. The service starts at 9.45 but we have a special time of prayer for half an hour before. I like that so much and really miss it when I can't go. Then we meet everyone in church. We have beautiful worship. We celebrate birthdays and anniversaries. We have many projects like kids club and for teenagers. And the preaching is very good.

Do you have any relationship or connection with the missionaries living in your city/town/area?

Yes

What do you feel about their involvement in the churches?

It is good that they come and help because they know so much about Jesus and they teach us new things, so we can learn from them. Also they are a good example to us. Here there is a lot of gossiping, the Bengali church is one way, but when the foreigners come we can see they are very open and not critical; they act a different way.

What are some of the common cultural mistakes or misunderstandings foreigners make in your country?

The biggest thing I have seen is that foreign couples, when they come into church and sit down together and are hugging during the preaching, it is distracting and you end up looking at them and not listening to the sermon. One more things is, if we are together and say having breakfast together or drinking tea and someone else comes in we offer some of the food or drink to them, but foreigners do not offer their food or drink. Of course it is their culture and ours is different so it doesn't make me upset, but any Indians meeting foreigners for the first time would be, especially villagers.

How do you feel about their levels of understanding concerning your culture and context?

I think they have good understanding on the superficial things but don't have a good understanding of our deeper things, for example our rituals. When a Hindu dies there are rituals that happen for the first ten days, and after one year. There are many rituals that happen when someone gets married.

If there was one aspect of your culture you would like them to know before they came to this country what would that be? (Why is this important for you?)

Relationships are very important to us. So when we arrange to see a foreigner and they cancel, it makes us feel very bad because we don't do this. If we are very sick or someone dies we will cancel, but otherwise, even if work suddenly comes in, we will cancel the work but not the visit. We are busy and we have relationships. Our busyness doesn't take place of our relationships. And we always keep in touch with each other, so even if we go to some other place, maybe to visit family, we will still phone each other and find out what how things are, what news they have. But foreigners don't do this. We don't have big gaps between visiting each other. And if, say, a foreign friend gets sick I want to go visit them and see how they are; but I think maybe in their culture they don't do that so it causes upset for me.

When I first met foreigners, I thought they were like gods, and I felt scared that they would talk to me. But when they did talk to me I liked it so much and I thought, "Wow - god has come." I wanted to be with them and spend time with them and I was very happy. But after some time, I got used to them and realised they were not gods.

LUÍS – SPAIN

What do you want missionaries to know about what it means to work here?

The most important principles for the formation of missionaries start with a clear call and understanding, where applicable, that it's a call for the whole family to the specific field.

It's assumed that they come with the backing of a mission or church or group of churches, and that this person will have been praying about where in the world to go.

I have seen many people from all over the world who have come to Spain; most of them don't speak Spanish well or achieve high levels of competence in the language. This is a handicap when it comes to being able to do the work of a missionary.

Generally, there are two forms in the way the missionaries come:

To open a new mission work or,

To become part of an existing church and collaborate with an existing church.

For those without the language, it is difficult to integrate into local churches and the local field. These people feel excluded or out of place because they don't understand the sermon or have the possibility of speaking with people after church, unless there is someone who speaks a little bit of English.

The process of learning the language is not the same for a child as it is for an adult. The child will find it much easier, and if they are in the local school they will also naturally have friends around them and therefore exposure to the language.

And many times missionaries meet with others of the same culture or language which causes them to have more difficulty in learning the language.

It's not the same - learning the language in a school as opposed to learning it on the ground here. It's different here, and the person needs to learn the customs of the place and the culture. Even in Spain things are completely different from province to province. It's hard enough for those of us from here, so how much more for someone who is coming in from outside. So the first thing that the person needs to have clear is to where God is leading them in Spain. Then the person should investigate the culture, the spiritual traditions of that place; and learn about the character of the people there, because of the differences inside Spain. It's important not just for the learning, but also has application at the point of gospel ministry.

The error most evident in the missionaries who come here is the lack of language that most people of Anglo-Saxon origin have, and the difficulty of learning it for some. Spain is very different from their culture; the humour of a British person is different from a Spanish person, and the way a North American sees the world is different from how a Spanish pastor sees the world.

Missionaries should seek to become part of the local church leadership, together with the local pastors. Of those who come, many missionaries end up burning out because they don't fit in the new church, because they feel alone, or because they feel separated from their extended family and their home church. Also, they may feel isolated because of how things are done locally. Many of these things discourage the person because they don't fit.

Aside from the language, the most important thing is to fit well into a local church where they go - to feel like they're not a foreigner but part of the local congregation. This depends heavily on the leadership of the local church. The local pastor can't see the missionary as a threat (because he wants to take his place or perceives he can do it better), or as someone who has come to make their work more difficult; but instead as someone who has come to support and give. It's not seen as a threat when the person who comes is a spiritual person and is one who comes to serve and join the local leadership.

When a person comes to serve, they serve; but when the person comes to "be something," that's when the problems start. So local pastors are threatened by the arrival of new people; therefore, it's important to tread carefully and slowly early on. The base of relationship with the leadership, not just the congregation, is vitally important in this. And missionaries need to know what their place is, too - within the congregation, with the family, and as part of the leadership. In this way it eliminates many potential fears.

So the missionary needs to understand where they fit and understand how the leadership sees that they are here to serve and help, not to do things according to how they perceive they should be done.

One thing that has always intrigued me in the past is that the majority of missionaries went to the south - because of the sun, the character of the people, and because there are more missionaries there to join. Some missionaries come with a clear idea to plant a church, some come to work with the existing church. Both are ok. The one who comes to open a church by himself is going to have a harder road. But I think the local churches need help and support, and if a mission came and asked me to collaborate, I would love to. I like the connections between missions and churches because we can work together toward sending a family to a particular area. I prefer the missionary to enter through the local church and we decide together how and when the person goes out to plant a church.

We also need to be focussing in on cities, not just towns because they are smaller and more difficult.

The most important things to have in place if the church wants to send out missionaries is the trust between people - that we have prayed for a long time about where to go and that we're all on the same page.

Then we would support them with their projects. And we need to have things clear before we start, because sometimes we have set up a new church or work and then the missionary has broken the relationship.

The missionary needs to have in mind that they are going to reach people of that language - Spaniards in this case. The Spanish are culturally reticent to listen to the North American. So the person needs to build relationships and friendships. They should be open to their children going to parties and relating to others; this will break down the barriers and make way for the message. So even though the Spaniard will struggle to listen to the message from someone from outside, it can happen if the bridge of a relationship exists. It even happened to me coming from the south of Spain. The Asturian doesn't let just anyone into their circle; and so the relationship bridges the gap. The Asturian won't give their heart to just anyone. Once you have their friendship, be very careful you don't betray them!

If I were to speak to prospective missionaries, the first thing I would say is, are you sure? Or is it a feeling or a prophecy? Because the calling needs to come first. And secondly, you need to be sure about the place where you are going. Then be clear about the price that you are going to have to pay, leaving so many things and also taking your family to a place that is new and strange.

And once they arrived I would want to say: Be patient. Observe. Watch how the people behave. Don't place your criteria on the situation. Be humble. Pray a lot. And then trust to be able to sow.

HOLONOU – TOGO

Where were you born, your family and your education etc...?

I am Togolese, born in Lomé in a family of 6 children including 4 girls and 2 boys. By the grace of God, all my Dad's children went to school, although some at a certain age decided to quit their studies despite the insistence of our

> *There are serious Christian churches, but there are also churches that are there only for business. They only make noise, all they want is people's money.*

parents to continue their studies. I did my primary, secondary and university studies in Lomé. Currently I am married and mother of 3 children including two girls and a boy.

Where did you go to school?

I did my primary classes at the Catholic Primary School of Dogbéavu, where we lived. After my primary school, I went to Junior High school at CEG Bè-Atikpa in another neighbourhood, which is a neighbourhood next to Dogbéavu (where I went to primary school). I continued Senior High school at the Lycée d'Agbalépedo and Plateau College. I continued my university studies at the University of Benin (Current University of Lome). I am currently studying theology courses at ESTAO / WAAST.

Are you employed and if so, what are you doing now?

I am a missionary 2001 in Pioneers-Africa, in charge of Child Protection.

Are you married? How did they meet and get married? Kindly share your story.

I am married. My husband and I were in the same church, on the same committee, the youth committee, and that's where we met. After a year and a half of engagement, we got married.

Do you have a relationship or connection with the many foreign or foreign NGOs that came to work in your country?

I have friends in foreign NGOs but myself, I have never worked in one of the foreign NGOs of the place.

What do you think of these different groups?

In my opinion, they help us. They help on many levels, they do good to the people.

What are the traditional belief systems of your culture and how do you feel about them?

We have Islam (myself, I am Muslim), Christianity, animism, atheists etc. With these different beliefs, I do not have problems especially with Christians. I'm comfortable with them. We eat together. We talk. In fact I have many Christian friends. By cons I do not really have friend animists. It's not that I have a problem with them, but I feel better with Christians than with animists and other religions.

What do you think of Christian churches in this country?

There are serious Christian churches, but there are also churches that are there only for business. They only make noise, all they want is people's money. So we have two kinds of churches in the country: serious churches and non-serious ones.

How did you meet Jesus? Share your story briefly.

I was raised in an animist family with a father well anchored in animism. It was forbidden for the whole family to set foot in a church where the Holy Spirit works. So we grew up as animists. One day my little sister and my cousin went to a church named Great Commission against Dad's advice of course. Every time they came back from the church, I made fun of them. But as I mocked, I noticed a joy in my sister; she spends her time singing hymns that made me laugh but at the same time I wanted to share the joy she had. One day, armed with courage, I decided to follow them to see what gave them so much joy. Arrived at the church that day, after a warm moment of praise, I decided to give my life to Jesus.

What kind of church do you attend? Describe a typical service.

I am a member of the church of the Great Commission International of Togo. I am part of the praise team. Typical Sunday service: there is an intercession time of one hour each Sunday, from 7:30 to 8:30. At 8:30 the worship proper begins with a time of praise. Then we have Sunday school followed by special songs (choir, band or fanfare). After that comes the moment of voluntary donations and offerings. After a time of worship, we move on to preaching followed by a small moment of prayer. The worship ends with an announcement time and end prayer at 11am.

Do you have a relationship or connection with missionaries living in your city / town?

Yes, Pioneers works in collaboration with other existing missions in the field.

How do you feel about their involvement in churches?

There are missions that understand that the mission needs the church; but others, though might understand, do not want to reach out to the churches.

What are some of the common cultural mistakes or misunderstandings foreigners make in your country?

The misunderstanding between the population of the North and the population of the South; the southern population considers the northern population to be inferior.

What are some of the areas of conflict that you observe among the foreign community?

There are often rivalries among some communities.

Where do you feel this arises from?

Selfishness and pride

What do you feel about their levels of understanding of your culture and context?

They understand that they need respect for our culture and for the Togolese population as a whole

If there was one aspect of your culture you would like them to know before they came to this country what would that be? (Why is this important for you?)

Respect for the Togolese population. The Togolese so much respects the stranger that he sees himself denigrated by the stranger. The stranger must know that it is not because he is so respected that he must be respectful.

TIMOTHY – SE ASIA

I hope when new missionaries come, they're like Paul who became "all things to all men." It's kind of like the adage, "When in Rome do as the Romans do." You need to know the people you're coming to serve. For example, there's a

> I've seen foreign workers being territorial about local believers.

big gap between the rich and poor here. Are you coming to serve people in the countryside? Or migrant workers in the city? Or the urban middle-class? Or the rich? These groups each have different lifestyles. People in the countryside tend to be a more practical; they also feel inferior. If you display a lifestyle different from theirs, they will feel that gap and won't open their hearts to accept you. They may question, "is this Good News only good for people like you, and not for me?" You must expect to adjust yourself to the needs and lifestyle of the people you serve.

You see, every culture has different ways of doing things, and I'd want to share with you how we do things here: how to make friends, what we eat, and even simple but profound differences like room and board. Differences in food are easy to predict, but they might not know that in the countryside, it's common for men to sleep with men, and women with women—not in a sexual way, just sharing beds. Since western people tend to be more accustomed to private space, this might feel strange. You must come ready to let go of many of your habits and ways of thinking.

But lifestyle is not the only consideration. You also need to know the local culture, its background and challenges. For example, people worship their ancestors here, and pantheism abounds; they believe in this god and that god. You might share with them a New Thing, and they say, "Good, good!" and believe, but underneath they continue their own beliefs. If you know this ahead of time, you can learn to share in ways that help people see that God is above all and he hates evil. He is not just one of many. I share this because of what I've experienced in our churches. When new people come to faith, at first they're very positive about it, but then after some time they don't connect with the teaching and they stop coming. When you're sharing, therefore, it's good to have an understanding of this and find ways to "filter" for people who are genuine and those who just appear to be.

Working with the local church can be a great thing. I'd encourage new workers to clearly define goals and do so together with the locals. In this way, they can work together better and be more fruitful. Otherwise, there may be conflicts. I've seen some unfortunate things. I've seen foreign workers being territorial about local believers. "These are mine, and those are yours." They may contact each other and say, "Can I do such-and-such with one of your people?" Respect and politeness are good, of course, but when the locals find out about this, they feel used. Another common problem is too much emphasis on results and whose results they are. It leads to suspicion about one another's motives and generally gets in the way.

However, partnering is good! Here are some good ways to do it:

It's undeniable that foreigners attract people, and I think this fact ought to be used well for evangelizing. But it's best in partnership with local brothers and sisters. Give the local church time and freedom to follow-up with new believers, but at the same time don't just hand over the person and leave. The missionary should maintain a role of encouragement and guidance for the new believers. They may need time to get used to the local church culture, and the foreign friend can support them through this.

Another helpful area of partnership is in biblical foundations. Foreigners come from places rich in resources for biblical training. In my hometown, however, we have much less, and thus the church there is conservative, fearful, and timid. So please, come train, and share resources. This helps a lot!

I hope that new missionaries are able to evangelize well, but that's not enough. They need to know how to disciple. They need a solid foundation in theology and biblical truth. And they need to have depth of character.

You need to be ready truly to live out your faith through your attitude. We know, of course, that the Bible teaches this, but it's difficult to do in a new and different environment. You might think and say you're humble and ready to identify with local people, but in your heart, there is still pride. It's understandable, for those from economically prosperous nations naturally tend toward this sense of superiority. You might not admit you have it, but local brothers and sisters can see it; it comes out of us in habits and ways that are difficult to change. Mature local brothers and sisters can handle this, but new believers may struggle. They have not yet learned to imitate Christ and will naturally follow others' examples, including yours. This is why Jesus told us that we are the salt and light of the earth; we must cultivate the attitude and character fitting for people of salt and light.

And I'd like to say something about commitment. We need to truly understand what our calling is. I personally am very careful to confirm my calling, because if we have a calling, it means we have a continuous, long-term responsibility to develop it and carry it out. This requires time and commitment. I've observed many who come from afar with great commitment, and it's very inspiring; it helps us see faith lived out. But we also see people for whom it's not clear if they were called or if they were simply trying to develop their career or respond to a work opportunity. I'm sure there's much I don't see, but without that strong sense of calling and corresponding preparation, it's easy to give up and go home. And that affects partnership with the local church.

Local brothers and sisters have often seen missionaries leave for lack of commitment and then have had to deal with the mess they left behind. Cross-cultural mission requires a clear sense of calling.

Look at the history of mission in my country. The reason there is such a precious and growing church in this country now is because of the commitment and sacrifice of the missionaries who came in the past. They gave their all. They became the seed that sprouted into the church. What amazing commitment! But those who just come for work or to have some "experience" tend to waste time and effort.

And lastly, clear calling alone is not enough. Some come, passionate and seemingly called, but their spiritual life seems shallow. It's as if all they know is one gospel presentation and that's their entire life. They don't seem to know much about the Bible. When they share their testimony, it's simple. They excel at playing games with young people, but when someone accepts Christ, they have no ability to disciple them, to give them spiritual food. So passion alone is not enough. There's nothing wrong with a simple testimony, but we need people to come and disciple us, feed us. Some of us first-generation Christians here have come through persecution and seen dramatic transformation. We are hungry for more; we need depth. When missionaries come who are deeply thirsty for the Word, know it well, and are truly committed to their calling, we are inspired. Please come with this readiness! To speak in local terms, come with not just a glass of water, but a whole bucket to give.

CELESTE – NATIVE AMERICAN

Because of their unique historical experiences, my people—the Tonawanda Band of Seneca—are quite independent. They succeeded in buying back lands that had been sold out from under them. They have established successful businesses

> *When Christianity first came to my people, it came wrapped up in white man's culture, and resulting churches had a white man's feel about them.*

(mostly smoke shops) which support families and tribal projects. They don't see themselves in need of much. They are a proud people and don't want the sympathy or interference of outsiders.

They are fiercely protective of their cultural identity and view Christianity as something completely "white"—something that robs them of their own identity. When Christianity first came to my people, it came wrapped up in white man's culture, and resulting churches had a white man's feel about them. Today there are few churches that exist among the Seneca.

Even though I am a member of the tribe, I'm not welcome to share with others about my relationship with Christ. My people are suspicious and believe Christians always have ulterior motives. I've decided that the way to reach out to my Seneca family and friends must be very relational, with a lot of prayer behind it. Rather than share things outright I like to simply show them things by my life, to make them curious, and to let them ask questions. If I let them initiate any conversations it's much better, because then it's less threatening to them.

It's really important that any outsiders interested in building relationships with the Seneca recognize it's just like going to another country. They need to understand major differences that exist between their culture and the culture of the Seneca people, and not expect the Seneca to conform to them. In the past (and still today) people expected the Seneca to adapt to the cultural ways of the outsiders. Instead, any Christians wanting to reach out to my people have to go as learners, not as teachers. They can't just walk in and expect to have a voice.

The tribe doesn't allow Christian workers on the Reservation, so more creative approaches will have to be taken. Anyone attempting a relational form of long-term outreach among the Seneca must know it will be a very slow process. They must do it prayerfully and carefully, as many of my tribe are very aggressive, see Christianity as bad, and don't want this foreign religion to spread among their people.

I would love to see what Seneca believers would look like if Jesus came to live among them and shared His ways and His truth with them. If the core truths of salvation (not packaged up in any outside culture) were shared with them I think Seneca worship of Jesus would be very beautiful and creative. I really don't know what true Seneca worship of Jesus would look like, but I do know it wouldn't look like the imposed form of Christianity we've experienced to this point.

CARLOS – PORTUGAL,

What do you want missionaries to know about what it means to come and work in Portugal?

One of the more crucial things is the need to "nail the language" – work on the language. In this it is important for

> *You learn the culture by living it, by seeing and experiencing problems and difficulties that the locals face.*

missionaries, where they can, to try and understand what environment would help them learn the language best - whether that be more academic setting (e.g., language course at a university), one-to-one tutoring, conversations with locals, etc., or a combination of these and other options.

It is also important for missionaries to understand that the Portuguese people are very traditional, and that a lot of their "tradition" comes from and through the Catholic Church. In the mentality of the majority of Portuguese, to be Portuguese is to be Catholic. It is common for a Portuguese person to think "We belong to the Catholic church before we believe…We're born into it."

It is not uncommon for the Portuguese to rebel against this tradition - and tradition in general - as a youth. However, many Portuguese come back to the traditions of the church as young adults.

Missionaries to Portugal also need to understand that "the idea of the mediator in the Roman Catholic sense is still very present inside of the evangelical church." Instead of the priest filling that role, though, it is now the pastor.

There are several things that result from this idea. Firstly, there is a lack of involvement by lay people in the church. It is expected that the pastor/leader will do everything. Secondly, there is a lack of discipleship, because the only person expected to do discipleship is the pastor/leader. Thirdly, many within the church don't see themselves as needing to serve the church.

Another thing to be aware of is that many young people in Portugal are becoming more liberal/embracing liberalism. This is evidenced in part by the way that many in Portugal accept and embrace the current Pope, who gives them tradition but also allows elements of liberalism inside the church. This appeals to the many Portuguese who want religion (want to feel like they belong to a religion), but at the same time don't want that religion to limit their liberties or the way the view the world.

Many of the leaders in the evangelical church in Portugal are not theologically trained. This has a big impact on pastoral work that is done, and also on the teaching and preaching of the Word. This can, and historically has, led to various problems within the church that otherwise might easily be avoided.

One thing that we want missionaries to do is inspire Portuguese people to serve God, to be involved in the city [in which they live], with the means that we have. In other words, it's important that missionaries don't alienate themselves culturally, but rather assimilates into the local culture.

The missionary should avoid letting the Portuguese church become dependent on getting resources from abroad, especially financial resources. This often results in the church not learning how, and not even expecting, to support their own workers, which in turn impacts the church in various ways including the level of financial giving, the mission focus of the church, etc.

The Portuguese people in general are often very welcoming, but not particularly open and honest, especially when face-to-face with someone. This cultural reality is often seen inside the church as well.

Another thing to be aware of is that there is not a lot of trust in church leaders inside the evangelical church. This in part probably stems from a lack of pastoral care and discipleship within the church.

How would you like to see new people relate to/partner with your church?

Don't hold back in sharing with the church where you stand theologically. Make sure that you also become aware of where the church that you're going to stands on theological issues. Try to know and understand the "hot" theological issues going on in the church/denomination/area. Try also to be aware of and understand the expectations that the church has of you, the missionary.

Be open and honest with the church, and allow the church to be open and honest with you. Ask questions, inquire about things related to the church – how things function, and even why they function the way they do.

Plan to stay long term, where possible. In Portugal it is often hard to "get things done" over the short term.

Get to know the culture. Be aware of the fact, as well, that there are differences in culture between the different geographical regions in the country.

Be aware that there are divergences between the evangelical churches in Portugal (it's not one homogenous bunch). There are some who will seek to secure the support of the missionary, to have them on "their side."

Challenge the bad things in the Christian culture in a positive way.

Be patient! The Portuguese get defensive easily. Change is slow.

How does a missionary "learn/understand" the local culture?

One of the first things to recognise is that there is a lot "under the surface" in the Portuguese culture. So, spending time with Portuguese people, observing the way they do things/how they interact is important. It takes time!

You learn the culture by living it, by seeing and experiencing problems and difficulties that the locals face.

As a missionary there can be the temptation to socialize/interact exclusively, or almost exclusively, with other missionaries/foreigners. This can be detrimental to learning the local culture.

There are things that outsiders can see in the culture and in the church that locals might be blind to. The missionary might be able to challenge/point out some of these things with the aim of helping the local church. Missionaries can "earn the right" to do this by immersing themselves in the language and the culture. If someone makes a concerted effort to learn the language and culture they will often earn the respect of locals, and consequently sometimes their "ear" as well.

Something that always goes a long way is serving and loving the people. When the Portuguese perceive that the missionary really loves and cares for them they will be more open to listen to that missionary.

What do you think is the most important thing for a foreigner to understand about your culture/people?

One thing that is good for a missionary to know is that the Portuguese (church) culture is open to missionaries. The church is used to having missionaries around.

Another important thing to understand is that the Portuguese are very traditional, although they don't often like to label themselves that way. This "tradition" comes through especially strongly when the Portuguese perceive that they are being attacked (they get defensive).

It is also important to keep in mind that to be Portuguese is to be Catholic. As such, many in Portugal are familiar with religious language and terminology. The missionary should feel free to engage a

Portuguese person on the subject of religion, and even challenge them on it.

What are the most important characteristics/traits that a missionary should possess?

One of the most important traits that a missionary should possess is patience. Things take a while in Portugal – making friendships, learning the culture, etc.; so patience is essential.

The "you scratch my back, I'll scratch yours" mentality is very big in the Portuguese culture. In light of this it is important for the missionary to be honest and transparent.

It is also important for the missionary to stand up for being a Christian. They'll need to be strong in their convictions and stand up even within the church, for what they believe God wants for them and His people.

ATSU – GHANA

Tell me your story: where you were born, about your family and upbringing etc....

I was born in Anlogah, in the Volta Region of Ghana. My father was polygamous—had 4 wives. My mother was the first wife. She had 5 children with my father. My father had twelve children in all from the 4 wives. I was

> *If a person is important to you, you want to spend time with him/her and let him/her know that... You want to find out about his/her household, farm, animals—the whole person.*

brought up in a very rural setting, on the farm. My parents were farmers and traders. Life was really tough growing up

Where did you go to school?

I started school when I was about 5 years old in the village. An uncle of mine who was living in the city later brought me into the city to stay with him and continue my education in Secondary school after which I went to the Teacher Training College.

Are you employed and if so what are you doing now?

I am a trained basic school teacher. I teach at one of the Ghana Education Service Schools. I also make time to do some "buy and sell "business to supplement my income.

Are you married? How they met and got married? Kindly share your story.

I met my wife in College. We were in the athletics team together. She was a very impressive sprinter, winning most of her races with ease. It was her dedication and commitment to her training regimes that drew me to her. Added to that was the fact that we were from the same ethnic group, spoke the same vernacular, loved the same types of food (which she prepares so well), were in the same profession which meant we could help one another excel, and my parents were excited about her.

Do you have any relationship or connection with the many foreign NGO's or foreigners that have come to work in your country?

Yes, we have a number of them come to help in our schools.

What do you think about these different groups?

Some of them are very hard working and love our people. We understand and appreciate the fact that many of them are having to make great sacrifices to leave their beautiful home countries (I have not been to any yet.) to come live and work among us. There is this medical doctor who has been working in our village for years now, so humble, so caring. He has saved several people from death. That generation was great. Unfortunately a good number of the new ones come in with an attitude. They think they know more than we, the so called locals, do in everything and they try to put us into their type of mould. They spend all their time on their computers and phones. One wonders what they are looking for. We have several beautiful places where they could go take pictures for example, but they seem only to be interested in pictures of naked children walking our streets and the many huge refuse dumps. I am told many of them use those to make great stories to help them get money for their lavish way of life in our country. Look for example at how they have managed to get our people to think, speak and dress like them. You pastors think for example that your Christianity must be robed in Western type dresses to look authentic, some of the reasons you will never have some of us with you.

What are the traditional belief systems of your culture and how do you feel about them?

Love and respect for elders and foreigners, (you could be dealing with your god without knowing when you are dealing with foreigners) and that is why we have a lot of respect for these foreigners but what are they giving us in return. Look at what these Chinese for example are doing to us, destroying our environment through illegal mining etc.

We also believe in very strong family ties. We are collectivists. In fact, but for that, some of us would not have been through school. Unfortunately, we are fast losing some of these belief systems, thanks to your modern education system. Do you really want me to go on with my rant? Hmm, I will rather pause here.

What do you think about the Christian churches in this country?

Hello, I hinted at that in my earlier response above. They are doing some great stuff; taking care of widows and children, building and running great schools and hospitals etc. But they also have a lot of downsides. Look at the loud noise they make during their services. Don't you think that church is big business in our country these day? I know a man who went for a loan to start a church very certain he will pay the loan in no time and become rich. People are preaching everything and asking for money to do their so called God's work. Hmm, time will tell.

What are some of the common cultural mistakes or misunderstandings foreigners make in your country?

Throwing money at people because they are perceived to be poor; - Teams should learn to work with their local partners and stop doing their own thing in the name of helping people.

Refusing to allow their local partners to lead- We have great leaders here, people who understand our situation and would be better leaders if allowed to. Many foreigners just don't see why they should not be in the lead at all times even if they don't understand the context they are working in. Simply put many foreigners just will not serve under local leadership.

Not appreciating our challenges and so not managing what they are given well- We had a team stay with us in one of our villages. All they wanted was American type food and the like. One day they asked for a number of stuff including American standard peanut butter spread. That meant a few hours' drive to the nearby supermarket which we gladly did. To our surprise, they quickly "wasted" all the paste in no time and were looking up to us to drive to the supermarket again for more when we had several other things doing.

If there was one aspect of your culture you would like them to know before they came to this country what would that be? (Why is this important for you?)

Greeting. Greeting takes time in our culture, it shows you care and want to know about the whole person. Just a flying good morning or good day is not enough. If a person is important to you, you want to spend time with him/her and let him/her know that… You want to find out about his/her household, farm, animals—the whole person. Learn the greetings and take time to follow through.

CHANDAN – INDIA

Interviewer's note:

I have known Chandan (name changed) for about 6 or 7 years and have seen him grow so much from the time he first came to my church as an intern. He is a Bengali from a Hindu background and is one of the assistant

> *I have interacted with so many people and sometimes people from other faiths are better human beings than Christians.*

pastors of my church in India. Although still in his 20s, he has a love of God, a heart for Bengalis and a gift of preaching that show a maturity beyond his years. He is married and he had a half-arranged/half-love marriage to a pastor's daughter, also Bengali. We sit in the church office ready to conduct the interview, enjoying a cup of chai (Indian tea) which I have come to love, with tropical-sounding birds serenading in the background, giving the illusion that we are in a village and not a bustling city of millions.

Tell me your story: where you were born, about your family and upbringing, etc....

I come from a Hindu background and it was a long journey searching for the truth for us. We were not really intentional about searching for the truth because we were quite happy and satisfied with our life; it was a very comfortable lifestyle. And I think that is what is interesting, because for me personally it's very unique. Most of the time we hear testimonies where God has made a drastic change in somebody's life, lifts them up from the pit. But I think God is also very relevant to someone who lives a very comfortable life, and for me and my family it was just like that. God is relevant to people who think they are happy, who think they are satisfied; He just does that because He brings a new perspective. So for me and my family that is how it was; it was a very long journey that started in 1993. My Dad got baptised in 1997. My sister and I were baptised in 2002. So you can see it was a pretty long journey for us. We are glad that God didn't just give up on us, that the pastors who worked in our family did not give up on us, and that they were patient for 10 years.

I did my schooling in a Catholic school because my Mum was also teaching there. So basically the only reason I was admitted into the school was because of my Mum, because I did very badly in my interview, and in my written exam...I didn't answer anything. The principal came and told that to my mum, saying, "We'll take your son basically because you are a teacher here; otherwise we wouldn't have taken him." Then I studied at the Don Bosco School which was run by Catholics, and did my college at St Saviour's, also run by Catholic priests.

Was going to Catholic school a factor in becoming a Christian.

It may have had an impact, God may have used it along with other things. The person I am today was shaped by the school and seeing the priest. But it's hard to be specific on exactly what God used to bring me to faith.

How did you meet Jesus? Share your testimony briefly with me.

My Mum actually came from a Christian background but she was not really serious about her faith. She lived like a Hindu anyway, and in Bengali families they have a lot of respect for Jesus; so we grew up basically believing all gods and goddesses, thinking they are all the same. We had pictures of every god in our house. But my attraction to Christ happened through a Hindu priest.

My Dad had just built a second level to our house and he wanted to do a house warming so he invited the Hindu priest. Before the pujas started we had all the pictures of gods and goddesses laid before the priest and the priest was about to start when he looked up and saw the picture of Jesus and said, "Hey, you guys believe in Jesus?" And my Dad said, "It's not like we believe in Him but we think that He is also a great god and so with all the gods we worship Him." The Hindu priest said to bring the picture down because - this is the answer he gave - "There is no other god greater than Jesus and no worship is complete without Jesus." And so my Dad apologised that he didn't know all these things, and he went and got the picture of Christ down. When the worship started the priest started by putting a tika on the picture of Christ, then he went to the other gods and goddesses.

So, as a young guy (teenager), I was looking at it and thinking, "Wow, we got it right - we had this picture of Christ, and the priest is saying He is greater than any other god." So that is how my attraction to God started. Looking back, I don't know if the priest really believed what he said or whether God was just using him to speak to me. The priest is still alive, and he's still a Hindu. Years later there was a pastor through different connections who came to our family. He asked if he could come and pray with us. And we were like, "Yeah, yeah, sure…" and I remember thinking he's the priest of the greater God, Jesus.

This pastor came to the family and he started coming weekly and just did a weekly Bible study with us. We would sit for the prayer and when he left we would continue with our pujas and all the other festivals. But I think it was slowly and gradually that it happened. For me, I thought I was a great guy and that the gods were very pleased with me and would bless me. But one verse that really spoke to me was from Isaiah were God says, "I'm so holy that all your righteous acts are like filthy rags in front of My holiness." That really contradicted my worldview because I thought I was great and gods were pleased with what I was doing. Then this God of the Bible says my righteous acts are filthy rags before Him.

It was then that I understood that I needed Him. I needed His grace, just by my work and righteousness I could not achieve it. And so that journey started and so eventually, through the proper systematic study of the Word of God, God really revealed Himself to me and to my family. It's interesting because for me and my family we had the same events happening but the experiences were so different; God spoke to us all in different ways.

What type of church do you attend?

The church I attend is fairly new; we just completed 10 years last October and this is our 11th year running. It's a church that is very mission-minded and I think that is one of the reasons it attracts a lot of people that are involved in missions or are serious about missions. It's a church that believes in partnerships, recognising that we are all working together for God's kingdom, not for ourselves or our empire-building. It's a multi-lingual church; we have Bangla, English, everything happening together, and I think that's one of the good things about it. There are different people coming from different backgrounds, and yet there is so much of fellowship that happens.

Do you have any relationship or connection with the missionaries living in your area?

Yes.

What do you feel about their involvement in the churches?

For us in our church, one of the things we are very clear and intentional about is that when we have expats coming in and when we have missionaries coming in, they are more involved in discipleship and equipping rather than outright evangelism. It's not like we tell them not to be involved in evangelism, because God does bring opportunities in everyone's life and it's on us whether we grab the opportunity or let go of it. But I think for us as a church we are intentional about being more equipping- and discipleship-orientated rather than being evangelistically-orientated. It doesn't just apply to foreigners coming in; even we nationals say when going to a village we try not to do evangelism by ourselves, we let the field workers handle it.

The field workers are there every week; they know the people. So even as nationals when we visit our fields we are very intentional and sensitive about not pushing it too much, but just to use it as a time to encourage people - the seekers that are coming as well as the new believers. We leave the evangelism to our field workers because they know the context; they know the people. And I think evangelism becomes better when it becomes more relationship-orientated rather than more assignment-based. My friend will not be offended if I share my faith with him, knowing that Nilav doesn't mean bad for me, he wants the good for me because he knows me – he's grown up with me.

So you think it is a good thing to partner with foreigners?

I think partnering with foreign missionaries is very important for India because God has blessed the global church. If a person from a particular church is called to come and bless another church then I think that has to happen. So there is a lot of value that gets added.

What are some of the common cultural mistakes or misunderstandings foreigners make in your country?

One is the social media. Sometimes when foreigners come they are too open about their involvement here on social media and that becomes very detrimental. We will now only partner with people who agree not to post what they are doing on social media.

The other thing I think - one of the dangers that I've faced - is that when foreigners come they feel that every opportunity should be an opportunity for evangelism, which biblically is also not right. When I see the book of Acts, Paul probably had the same idea, but God stopped him and in a dream gave him the Macedonia call. So I very strongly believe that not every opportunity is an opportunity for evangelism. That is something we need to be very sensitive about especially for an outsider when they come.

Another challenge is that they don't have proper orientation of the culture here and they start behaving like they would back home. It doesn't work here. You know, no.1: guys and girls can't stay together. They have, and people have noticed and they've come and complained, so we had to do damage control. Another is taking selfies. When you go to another country you just want to click pictures of any and everything, and the funny thing is when we visit their countries we are not allowed to do it. They say they like their privacy, but what about the people here? Just because they seem poor, you just click pictures. So there has to be a lot of dignity in the photos they take.

Also, Indians are very relational, so when they see people for the first time they want to come and talk to you and basically make you feel welcomed here. But sometimes what happens in cultures from another country, maybe that is not the norm there, maybe they like their space…they don't like being intruded on. So there have been instances where someone from church has gone to a new person, with good intentions, to make them feel included…and some of them have responded saying they felt very intimidated. Again, I think that is because people have not been orientated properly. Here people will comment on your height, your weight, your complexion - everything basically - not in a bad way; it's either approval or concern, never to put you down or to insult you. That is how Indians are, so I think a lack of orientation…or maybe people are stubborn and just don't want to listen!!

What are some of the areas of conflict you observe among the foreign community?

I think 99% of our involvement with foreigners has been amazing. God has just brought people that fit with the ethos of our church; they have agreed to our way of working. They have listened to what we have said and have come with a heart to serve, not with a heart to lord over everything. But there have been events where it has not happened so well. As a result, in those cases we don't partner with them anymore, because for me personally, I think friendship should come before any ministry involvement.

Ministry is not like a business contract, i.e., "This is my responsibility, this is your responsibility, you don't cross my line, I don't cross your line." That is not what ministry is to me. I think most of the partners we have, have had that kind of a flow. It has always been friends trying to work together, helping friends, without any desire to bring glory to yourself and stuff. We had a challenge with one person...I recognise that most missionaries when they come here, usually either through an organisation or a church, may come with a desire to bring their organisation along. When they want to work with us, we want to make it very clear what our church stands for. If they say in effect, "No, my organisation sent me, that name should come and that should be the focus, not your church. If you guys want our help, good; but if not, well..." And we say we can't work like that, so...That is a challenge when missionaries come and want to bring their organisation. It doesn't work here because the government is becoming all the more strict, and it is very foolish to do, but there are people who want that and so we say, "Sorry, we can't work like that."

How do you feel about foreigners' level of understanding concerning your culture and context?

One thing that I feel is, especially in India, the church here is growing. It's not like many people come from a Christian background, or who have been Christians for generations; a lot of people are new believers. The focus of the church, of the missions here, is more evangelism. And when we have missionaries coming in from other countries, I feel sometimes they don't understand it. It could be because of a cultural thing or whatever; maybe I would not understand their concept if I went to their countries. Even the teachings that they give are not relevant as such. I mean they might be great teachers of the Word back home, but because of the lack of understanding of the culture here, sometimes the teachings become very irrelevant.

We've had a lot of preachers come in, and now our field workers [Indian Missionaries] feel more comfortable with us because they have been working with us, some of them for the past 10 years. They just come and say, "You know what I feel? It was a waste of time." Now coming here for a missionary is very expensive and if you're coming here doesn't really add value to the ministry, I think you should reconsider. And I also understand the impact comes from God. God does it, but I think we also should be good stewards of the experiences or resources or finances or whatever is involved. It's not just coming here, saying something and going away feeling good about it, but seeing what the actual impact is.

So now for our church, with all the different partners that we have, we have tried to keep them focused on different areas. Recognising their gifts and talents, we encourage them to stick to that. At the end we recognise that there are times when God uses your weaknesses as well and we want to be sensitive to that.

If there was one aspect of your culture you would like them to know before they came to this country, what would that be?

I think sometimes in the church context when we look at people who are not believers - people from other faiths - we have this thing that they are in darkness and so they are evil. They are not evil!! They are sometimes better - morally, culturally better - than Christians. And sometimes when we have people coming in, that is what is in their minds: They are Hindus, they are in darkness, they are evil. They are not evil. I have interacted with so many people and sometimes people from other faiths are better human beings than Christians.

So I think that is something that if it is kept in mind can make a lot of difference, because at the end it's the love that matters. It's not what you say, your oratory skills or knowledge or experiences; people should know that you love them. "I am Hindu but they love me." And they should be open to that. I think that is a key thing. At the end it is God who brings conviction, it is God who changes lives and the problem happens when I don't respect someone else's worldview...thinking that you have to conform to my worldview because my worldview, my arguments are correct, my arguments are flawless.

Someone once asked me whether the eastern worldview that is more inclusive, or the western worldview which is exclusive - there is only one truth - is more biblical. I said "Neither." He said, "Why? Isn't it the western because Jesus is the only way, truth and light, it's like one truth?" "No," I said. "Neither is biblical. The eastern view says everything is true. That is not correct; you can't have multiple truths in a given time. But the western view is also wrong because the western view believes in exclusivity with pride, not with humility. It says, "I am right, you are wrong and you will listen to me!" which is totally wrong, the attitude is wrong.

YOUSEF AND MERYEM – MOROCCO

Interviewer's note:

Yousef has been a believer for 8 years. He is one of the leaders in the local church and meets with a group in his home. He is

> *The importance of prayer cannot be overemphasized.*

passionate about reaching the locals, but in his own words, he needs help. They live in the spiritual and religious capital of Morocco. They have been married for twelve years. They have two sons. His wife Meryem came to faith 3 years after he did. Both love the Lord and are solid in their faith. They are more economically independent than other believers. Yousef runs an import-export business while Meryem works at a local swimming pool.

My journey towards Christ:

My conversion had been a long process. Back in 2003, I accessed an internet site and learned about other religions such as Judaism, Christianity, Catholicism, Orthodox and Protestantism. However, knowledge about them did not help me. I was living an empty life and between 2006 and 2007, I was really restless. Towards the end of 2007, still searching, Christ took me by the hand and led me to Christianity. I emailed the pastor I knew from the French church. I started attending the church every Sunday, and there I prayed my first prayer. Like most people, when I opened my heart to Christ, I found out that He was actually already there waiting to take me in His arms. It was this knowledge of the great love of Christ that led me to Him and His marvellous kingdom.

No one talked to me about Christ. There were many pastors but no one understood my pain. So, I searched for people who could help me understand the Word of God. Later on, I got to know some missionaries, one of whom took me under his wing and helped me. What a difference that made! I discovered that faith is knowing God more and more till you see His majesty and grandeur; finding someone who can help you do that is a great gift.

My wife called my conversion a scandal. For three years, she had to live through that. By God's grace, however, she also came to faith. She always says that she converted because of people's prayers. You see, when my son got sick many people were praying for him. They were also praying for my wife because they knew our situation. After she accepted Christ, she came to know those same people. Their repeated profession that they had been praying for her had a deep impact on her. That is why she is fully convinced of the necessity of prayers.

Local realities:

Anyone who is led to come to Morocco must know a little of the history of Morocco, her culture, her people's way of life, how they behave and how they see Jesus. This is likewise true whichever city he ends up working in. He should also know a little about their struggles, their sufferings. A local person who can possibly act as his guide and tell him the truth about Moroccans will be a great help. This will provide him a reality check on what he has personally heard about and seen of the locals' daily lives.

For someone to be accepted, a knowledge of local traditions is valuable since Moroccans do not take kindly to someone who disregards cultural dictates; in common parlance, simply someone who "does not behave well." This comes side-by-side with the necessity of accepting the locals themselves and respecting their particular culture, which many times involves a sense of propriety and social protocols.

It is a common mistake for a foreigner to do things the way he does them in his culture. This creates problems. To avoid this kind of situation, the missionary should get to know the local people, sit down with and ask questions from them, even join in their traditional celebrations.

Moroccans are hospitable and they readily welcome foreigners. However, there is something about them that does not like authority. That is, someone who judges them or has authority over them. They do want to know about and understand the rest of the world, but that will be difficult if they sense that someone sits in judgment over them.

Moroccans also do not like people who show too much curiosity about their lives or give unsolicited advice. Hence, a foreigner must guard against entering too much into the problems of the family he knows.

In matters of faith, one must tread carefully. Here, families still stand united under one faith and they would not want to even hear that one of their members has converted to another faith. Thus, the missionary ought to know a little about Islam, how it is expressed in people's daily lives. Also, he should know how committed the person he is meeting with is to it. Questions like, "Is he a practicing Muslim?" "Does he faithfully go to the mosque or not?" will inform how he talks to the locals about his own faith.

One word of caution:

The missionary must endeavour to get to know the person he is meeting up with and establish a good relationship with him. He should avoid attacking Islam the first chance he gets. This is likewise showing respect for and accepting the local culture.

Reaching the locals:

It is crucial that the missionary knows the Word of God and teaches it well. When God's Word is taught well and enters a Muslim's heart, it will do its role of moulding and softening. However, when the missionary teaches, he must be careful to open his Bible and talk to the locals from it, show them that what he is teaching comes from the Bible itself. Otherwise, the latter will lose interest.

Needless to say, he must know the language. Otherwise, how else can he communicate the truth? Here, people speak the local dialect – Daria – and Classical Arabic. Fifty to sixty per cent of the population can understand French. The missionary must reach a level of language that enables him to be God's mouthpiece among the people he has been sent to reach.

The importance of prayer cannot be overemphasized. Thus, before he even starts ministering to people, the missionary must water everything in prayer. He must have a group of people, the church itself praying for him. This is a discipline that he must never neglect.

The missionary must be a good witness. That is, his life must reflect what Jesus taught and what he himself teaches. He cannot sit on the opposite sides of the same fence. That is, he cannot teach the Word of God and live far from its truth. The contradiction will be obvious and the Moroccans or any Muslim for that matter will see it.

He must also be patient and give the person time to respond thoughtfully to anything he says. The latter cannot be hurried since there is no place for him to go where he can be alone and reflect on what he has just heard. The reality is, Moroccans do take a lot of time to open up and analyse events. They may receive an idea, but will not respond to it quickly. If they do, then something else is motivating them to do so. Is it his friendship with the missionary? Is it the thought of personal benefit?

Coming alongside the local church:

Frankly, any missionary who comes to Morocco must love the church. He must pray for the church and see where believers are in their Christian faith. The reality is, the members of the local church all come from a Muslim background and that means that is where they draw from when they talk. The missionary then must approach the leaders or someone responsible for the church and ask relevant questions, like, "Can I participate in your service?' "How can I pray with, for you?" "What are the difficulties are you labouring under?" "How can I help this church grow?" This is how he can initially link up with not just one church, but all the churches.

He can be involved in the life of the church. However, this involvement has its boundaries. He is not here to take up a position in the church or be a member of the church. Rather, he is here to participate in the relationship-building and the growth of the churches here in the city. He is to evangelize, to speak the Word of God and help the church grow.

It will be good for the missionary to realize that his relationship must first be with the church, not the locals. Let me explain. If he has been meeting up with a Moroccan, say for a month or two, he will have established a relationship with him. If the Moroccan agrees to continue the relationship, the worker should orient the latter towards the Moroccan church and put him in contact with another Moroccan. Likewise, when he has led someone to Christ or knows someone who claims to be a believer, he should take the latter to the Moroccan church in whatever home the members are meeting. The worker must not try to take the Moroccan church to his home. He can pray with them; but he has to let the relationship of the Moroccan continue and remain with the Moroccans.

The reasons for this are practical. Realistically, because we are Moroccans, we can tell and know whether the person is sincere or not. Also, sometimes we tend to forget that the missionary/Moroccan relationship is limited. The missionary is here only for a short time; he cannot disciple a local from afar. In addition, past experiences have shown us that once the foreigner leaves, so does the Moroccan. However, when the Moroccan has a relationship with the church, chances are he will remain with the church. Furthermore, for a Moroccan to grow, he must be part of a community. This is what the church can provide and be – a community where he belongs, grows in maturity and exercises his spiritual gifts.

Building trust:

Trust is fundamental in relationship-building leading to gospel proclamation. Like I said, Moroccans are hospitable. They love people and welcome foreigners. This is linked to their opinion that because a foreigner comes to their country to do something, the foreigner can be trusted. Thus, when they open their door the latter, implicit trust is there.

Building on that initial human trust is the missionary's task. Strengthening it should follow suit and will depend on the foundation it is built on. Here, a knowledge of the culture and the people will go a long way.

Not everyone is the same; but, there are those who might think they can profit from a foreigner. It is not a remote possibility that someone may think, "This foreigner calls me, asks me to come to his place, eat and see a film about Jesus. I will go and ask him for money." It is thus essential that the worker reflect on how he communicates the message he wants to share and who he can share it with.

Similarly, zeal for the Gospel should not lead to imposition of it on a person. Sadly, a missionary can sometimes be oblivious to this fact. He may be sharing the Word to someone who cannot read or write and continues doing so to the point that the person feels that the missionary is imposing his faith on him.

Likewise, in his desire to reach others, he may take a person's silence as agreement. The person may be listening but he does not understand what the missionary is telling him. Yet, he will not say so. All he sees is a foreigner, someone who may help him get a job or give him something and his mind stops there.

Hence, in both cases, the missionary must be wise. He must always make an effort to understand what is happening beyond what he can see, and know how to deal with it. Trust cannot flourish on the sands of imposition and presumption.

Lastly, the missionary must walk his talk. This goes back to living out the Word he is preaching. It is not possible to take someone in, drink coffee with him, give him a Bible, tell him not to be afraid, and then pull back when trouble comes. The local person is watching and when he detects the disconnect between what he hears and what he sees, confusion can set in. "What is the missionary afraid of?" is a question that can rock whatever relationship the missionary has established with the local person he is reaching for Christ.

A recap:

Prayer is of utmost importance for anyone who seeks to serve the Lord in Morocco. Through it, the Lord can show him what he can possibly do to glorify Him here. He should serve the Moroccans through a life that reflects His presence. He must remember that he is here first as Christ's witness and must therefore tell people what Christ has done for him. As he relates with the church and with other believers, His love must radiate. When people see his love for God and that of the believers' for each other, the former will be interested in knowing the Saviour. Missionaries/workers, in a sense, are fresh winds of the testimony of Jesus Christ.

SONYA – BULGARIA

What do you think a missionary should know about what it is like to come and work here?

I think that above all the missionaries should love the country and the people with

whom they will work. The second very important thing is to be able to communicate in the local spoken language and to be financially independent.

Would you be more concrete?

What I mean by "love the country" is to know about the country's rich historical and cultural past and as a factor on the Balkans – for example, ethnical tolerance toward minorities such as the Roma, Muslims, Mohammedans and others.

What should the missionaries know about the worldview of the Bulgarian and its psyche?

Due to the total economical bankruptcy and the big percentage of unemployment, the majority of the people are very poor, low-esteemed and have the tendency to complain. As a result of this poverty people have servile behaviour toward foreigners, especially from West Europe and the US. In spite of that the people are hospitable, ready to help in need.

Is the Bulgarian language difficult and what are its peculiarities?

The Bulgarian language is a very rich one of the group of the Slavic languages and it's difficult for foreigners. There are genders and the grammar is difficult. The Russian language is very similar to the Bulgarian.

Would you say something about the country's traditional religion?

Historically Bulgaria is a Christian country since the 9th century. Traditionally Bulgaria is an Eastern Orthodox country. In the Orthodox Christianity the Bible has lost its authority, the icons and the Virgin Mary are highly esteemed, above Jesus Christ and His authority. The many pagan rituals and traditions which the indigenous religion practices are the focus of the so-called "Christianity" in Bulgaria. Because of all this the Bulgarian does not know Christ as "the Way, the Truth and the Life."

Are there other religions popular or known in Bulgaria?

The three major religions in Bulgaria are: Orthodox Christianity, Catholicism and Protestantism. The Muslims in Bulgaria are about 18% and many mosques have been built. It is encouraging to see some Muslims accepting Christianity. There is a network of small Protestant churches across Bulgaria. There are other religions such as Jehovah's Witnesses, Mormons, New Age and others.

Is the religion part of the educational system?

Religion is not part of the educational system in Bulgaria. This is somewhat fortunate since if it were, most probably the student would be taught the pagan rituals and traditions mingled in the country's religion. Lately, "Sunday school" has begun in some of the orthodox churches.

What is the attitude and opinion of the Bulgarian toward the evangelical Christian?

The ordinary Bulgarian does not know God and the Bible, therefore at Christian holy days demonstrates pseudo-Christianity. The missionary work is characterised as an anti-Bulgarian action, aggression toward the Orthodoxy.

How could the local evangelicals be of help to the missionaries?

One of the ways the local evangelical believers can be of help is by explaining the purpose of the missionaries' work; i.e., to point to the difference between religion and faith. This way they will help to neutralize the aggressive attitude from the Orthodox pastors.

Would you like to share your expectations of the missionaries?

The missionary's work is difficult and slow, often there are no visible results. I expect from the missionaries to reflect in their lives the vision they are following, to be accountable and cooperate with local evangelical Christians in the common goal. The missionaries would have to learn to work as a team with the indigenous evangelicals. They have to be honest and passionate toward the problems of the people they evangelise.

SAMPSON – GHANA

Tell me your story: where you were born, about your family and upbringing etc....

I was born in Agbozume in the Volta Region of Ghana. Raised in a polygamous family. My father had three wives. My mum divorced once, was rejected the second time and ended up in a third marriage. I was forced to live and grow up with my grandmother without parents' direct supervision.

> *The Western culture is very mechanical and strictly result oriented whereas African culture is slower with relationship valued over immediate result and accounting.*

Where did you go to school?

I went to Elementary School in my village, travelled to Keta Business College, did my Sixth Form in Tema Secondary School and ended up at the University of Ghana, Legon.

Are you employed and if so what are you doing now?

I am a missionary leader, mentor, and trainer who is focused on UPGs and cross cultural missions, mainly in West Africa.

Are you married? How they met and got married? Kindly share your story.

Married to Janet, a child evangelist, who I met on the job when I volunteered for the Ghana Evangelical Missions Association. Both of us have since been involved in church planting and mission work around West Africa.

How did you meet Jesus? Share you testimony briefly.

I was sick and dying when an auntie introduced me to a Christian fellowship where I was confronted with the claims of the gospel and I accepted Jesus Christ as Lord and Saviour.

What sort of church do you attend? – tell about a typical Sunday service

We start with intercession prayers, continue with one hour Bible study, follow with songs in a praise and worship session. The service continues with the sermon and teaching. We end up with announcement and guidance for the week's activities. Biblical African worship is the focus.

Do you have any relationship or connection with the missionaries living in your city/town/area?

We send and receive missionaries from the Northern sector of the country and some West African countries. We also have relationship with foreign missionaries who visit and work with us.

What do you feel about their involvement in the Churches?

They bring to bear on each church the mandate of the Great Commission. Anytime they are around we emphasize the call to duty. They remind us of reaching the unreached.

What are some of the common cultural mistakes or misunderstandings foreigners make in your country?

Most foreigners feel, or think, they already know enough about our communities through reading or some form of earlier contacts before arrival. They also presume that what worked with them will work in our context. Sometimes books are more trusted than live comments by practitioners on the fields. Sometimes practices of another culture are imposed unknowingly.

What are some of the areas of conflict that you observe among the foreign community?

Conflicts arise over financial matters very often. Timelines and deadlines are concepts which don't easily work out well. There is also misunderstanding over what is conceived as truth.

Where do you feel these arise from?

Sometimes we have misconceptions about cultural values. The Western culture is very mechanical and strictly result oriented whereas African culture is slower with relationship valued over immediate result and accounting. The African also is sometimes face-saving and not realistic enough about what is involved for instance in a given project.

How do you feel about their levels of understanding concerning your culture and context?

Most Westerners don't do their homework and are not patient to immerse for the sake of learning. There is a notion and presumption that they know enough.

If there was one aspect of your culture you would like them to know before they came to this country what would that be? (Why is this important for you?)

That our culture is dynamic - the values and norms are dependent on each given cluster of communities. Our culture is not mechanical and therefore cannot be derived from a set of assumptions. This is important because without patient learning, many mistakes can ruin an otherwise healthy relationship. Questioning given answers reveals the truth in a purported answer. On matters of financial integrity, adequate processes should be explored to ensure a fair chance is given to the African partners

DANIEL AND ESTHER – NORTH AFRICA

Interviewer's Note:

Daniel became a believer by watching the television program "Al-Hayat." Later on, he got to know a missionary and began meeting up with

> *They should be able to discern a true believer from one who is not. This may be a little tricky!*

him. Esther began following Christ three years later. They have a teenage daughter. The family lives in a neighbourhood where they are the only Christians. Daniel works odd jobs at a hotel. Esther sews traditional clothes, but the competition does not make it a profitable enterprise. These are not their real names.

"Who is Jesus? How can I have a relationship with God? People will call me a kufr if they know! How do I pray? God, give me someone who will show me how!" These thoughts were running through my mind during those times when I was searching for God. By His grace, someone contacted me by phone and advised me to get in touch with a missionary. I did. With the help of that man and his wife, I also got introduced to the bigger family of God.

Three years later, my wife came to faith. She always says it was because she saw the changes in me. For that, I give my Lord the glory.

The local church

There are very few believers in this city. Since the expulsion of 2010, things have changed. Nowadays, believers do not meet a lot. My family gets together with other believers for service every Sunday. It usually lasts for 3 hours, with 3 or 4 families in attendance. We meet at someone's place at around 6:00 or 7:00. We sit together, sing and study the Word.

Advice to new workers

For new people coming to work here, some things are indispensable.

If they want to succeed, it is essential that they know the culture. Understandably, there are differences between a foreigner's culture and ours. Nonetheless, it is a divide that can be bridged with the assistance of a local person who can help them understand its many facets and nuances. If they prove themselves honourable, that person will go to great lengths to help them.

Familiarity with local traditions, coupled with awareness and openness, is important. Here, there are things that people do not talk about because they are considered shameful. There are likewise codes of behaviour that are observed between men and women. Each family is different and their lifestyles are also different. However, there are rules that are heeded even among members of the same family. For instance, when a man enters the room, the women must don their fular (head covering) or their jellaba (a local long dress worn when women go out of the house, often over whatever they may be wearing when a man comes in).

Needless to say, as in other parts of the world, there are good, hardworking people here and there are those who are the exact opposite. Some can be very generous; others may charge foreigners higher, and a few may try to really rip them off. Newcomers must definitely be observant and sensitive.

They must find ways to establish relationships with people. This involves investing time to be with them, observing how they live and seeing them as "people" in their own particular situation. Discerning the right time to share their faith is part of this process. I would advise them not to do so at the beginning. Their primary concern at this point is to establish the relationship.

Undoubtedly, the ability to speak the language is essential. With that in mind, it is imperative that they should know how to talk to people about God. Although sharing the Gospel here is difficult, there is a great need for evangelists. However, they do have to exercise caution when they evangelize. That is, they do not have to share everywhere or to everybody, for obvious reasons. This is a Muslim country and for Muslims, believers are mushrikin (people who associate partners with God). We believe things about God that they consider blasphemous and are thus unacceptable.

It is vital as well that workers think about what they will do once they get here, and where they will live. It is advisable that they be engaged in something in order for them to live here. Starting up or doing a project will help them gain some credibility. At the same time, they must also have plans for when the initial project does not work. Moreover, they should not be fazed when difficulties come.

Some expectations and concerns

Since they are newcomers, they should endeavour to understand the faith of the local Christians, the believers' spiritual condition, and how they share their faith. Likewise, they must consider how they can work with the local believers to strengthen the church. In this regard, a few things need to be emphasized.

We would like them to relate to the church as a family. We would appreciate hearing testimonies of how they came to the Lord and learn from their experiences. Because of the current security climate, however, we should meet in the church. We cannot meet in the house because people are watching. In our case, when locals see foreigners in our house, they may become too curious and ask questions. We do not necessarily have to meet all the time or with everyone, either. The important thing is, we know each other and we can meet from time to time.

Because foreign workers come here as God's ambassadors, we regard them as ahead of us in terms of faith, as more mature, and necessarily, more knowledgeable. Thus, it is good if they can teach or give us lessons from the Word. They can also help those who are weak in their faith or those who have physical needs but do not have the means to meet them (e.g., no jobs).

If they want to work with the church, they should know the Bible. Similarly, they should be able to discern a true believer from one who is not. This may be a little tricky! However, a true believer is known to people, known in the church. For example, I am Daniel. They know that I am a Christian. They know I read my Bible and fellowship with other believers. How can one claim to follow Christ and do none of these things? He may have another purpose, other motives.

This is why it is not advisable to immediately introduce a new person to the group. For security reasons, we don't want to expose the members of the group to someone who can identify them later on, unless we are certain that the new person is really a sincere seeker. Besides, the new person likely does not know anything about the church yet, nor what it means to be a real follower of Christ in this context. So, the foreigner should take one or two local believers when he meets with the new person so they can also get to know the latter. The believers will be able to tell. Once they have ascertained the new person's sincerity and readiness, then they can bring the person to the group.

Lessons from the past

It is not only the state of things that has changed here; believers have as well. Some of them have made sacrifices and suffered because they love Christ. Needless to say, this is not true of everyone. However, we can personally testify that though we used to be afraid, we no longer are. Whereas before we used to be ashamed, now we are transformed. Christ has changed our minds and our hearts. He has used the things that happened and the difficulties we experienced to strengthen and show us that we can overcome. Yes, it is not easy to be Christians here; nevertheless, we have Jesus as Lord in our hearts and because of that, we are at peace.

FELIPE – BOLIVIA

Interviewer's Note:

Felipe began traveling with our family as we would do evangelism in rural areas

> *We all work for the same cause and goal.*

around Sucre, Bolivia. It was obvious that Felipe had a heart for evangelism, as he would come alongside people and share with them the good news. Felipe took these opportunities seriously. In fact, I would say that Felipe is a modern-day Apostle Paul and Barnabas, all wrapped up into one person.

Felipe preaches the Gospel and mentors and encourages the young pastors. We travelled together constantly and Felipe would preach and teach the Word of God as we distributed the solar-powered radios by the thousands. At one point a few years ago, Felipe expressed his desire to work with the children and present the Gospel to them while their parents were gathered hearing about the solar-powered radios. So I took over preaching the Word of God to the adults while Felipe would take the children to one side and share the Gospel with them. This is Felipe's passion now. He plants the Seed in their hearts while they are young and he trusts God that when they are older, they will never forget it. I consider it an honour to be Felipe's friend and brother in Christ but also to be mentored by him.

Tell me about your life - where you were born, about your family and the first years that you remember.

I was born on January 5, 1941 into a Roman Catholic family. My parents, who have both passed away, were Lucas Martinez and Afonza Martinez but they were in no way related or from the same family even though they shared the same last name. The last name "Martinez" had multiplied in the area and was brought to Bolivia by the Spanish. There are 3 communities in the area where the majority of the families have the last name Martinez.

I was brought up in a very Catholic family that was very superstitious. My parents carried on the belief in idols of their parents, with names such as Candelaria, Santiago and Santa Ana, and celebrated them each year. I remember the dates well. Candelaria's day was February 2, Santiago's was the 25 of the same month and lastly Santa Ana on the 26. They also believed in "Glory," an unknown god, Pacha Mama (the Mother Earth) and the spirits of the hills and mountains. To appease the Pacha Mama and spirits, they would present a sacrifice to them called the "q'oa" every week on Friday between 4 and 5 o'clock in the morning. They also believed that Pacha Mama lived in the middle of their yard.

According to the priests, all of the idols, Pacha Mamas, spirits and the "glory" were very powerful and were to be feared and respected. If we were to get sick, our parents would go and see the healer, or witch doctor, and he would tell them, "Your idol is angry." or "Santiago is angry because you did not do a celebration for him lately." or he might say that they had to go to the Catholic church in the city of Potosi and pay for a special mass for "Glory." This mass was celebrated by the priest there on the Sunday during Easter (Resurrection Sunday). Who was this "Lord of Glory"? He was different than the rest of the idols. He was the one they could not see or touch. I believe He was the Living and True God who they worshiped without knowing. I now realize that my parents also believed in the True God as did the Athenians without knowing like in Acts 17:23.

My parents, as I mentioned, were very superstitious. They believed in dreams, the birds, and specific things that would occur. For example, when my father dreamed about some cows, he said that that his plans were not going to work out very quickly but if he dreamed about horses, he was happy because his plans were going to come pass quickly. If he would dream about meat, this was bad because it meant that his plans would fail and it was in vain that he was even thinking about it.

Another example is that when he would be leaving the house and a man would pass by the front door, it was good luck for him; but if a woman happened to pass by, he would not leave the house that day because things would not go well for him.

My mother believed that the song of the birds spoke to her. She called the bird songs "wichico," "venti fue" and "pitilco." Each one had its specific tune and each one told her something different. Some brought good luck and some just told her that she could expect something surprising to happen. Depending on the tone, my mother found direction for her day. One I remember well was when she heard the pitilco sing "cusila, cusila," she said that my dad was coming home and he had some good news for us. I found myself as a child paying close attention to these birds and having my life guided by them. It was the same feeling back then as one has now when receiving a text message on their cell phone.

My father also knew how to read the stars. He knew their names. On June 4 or 5 he would look for some special stars that would tell him how the rest of the year would be. They would tell him to plant his crops early or to wait. For him, the stars never lied. He would look at the position of the new moon and tell if it was going to rain a lot that month or if the month would be dry.

Mixed into all of these beliefs was the memorization of prayers, including the "Our Father" prayer from Matthew 6:9-13. I remember that my grandfather had it written on a big piece of leather and that he would take it around to others in my village and teach it to them.

My grandmother told many stories from the Bible. She talked of men sent from God visiting us and that was why if a visitor came, it was important to offer them food so that God would bless our house.

Where did you study? Did you graduate from High School, attend university, seminary or a Bible Institute?

Around the year 1950, the Jesuit missionaries began to open the schools in Bolivia known as "Escuelas Cristianas" or Christian Schools. This is where I attended until grade 5 and learned to read and write. The schools only offered classes to this grade. I took a year off from studying; I was 17 by this time. It was in 1960 that my Dad sent me to an evangelical school in another town that was run by an American evangelical missionary. I finished grade 6 there but did not finish high school, let alone go on to university at that time.

What is your occupation?

I really did not have any occupation until the year 1968, even though I was 27 years old. I had tried such things as labourer, shoe maker, teacher, tailor and baker. Of the 5 things I had tried, my heart felt more inclined to being a teacher and working with children; this is what I ended up doing. I can see now that God had a plan and that He was showing me what He would have me do in the future for His glory. I suppose God tried to use my mother to tell me this. I can remember back to when I was 14 years of age and my mother would say, "I want to have a son who is a teacher. You are going to go to 'Caiza.'" This was the town where there was a teacher's college. These words of my mother are etched in my memory. I did not end up going to the teacher's college but I did work with children at the local schools for 4 years until 1964. I was a Christian at this point.

My desire to teach led me later to a Bible Institute in Sucre where I taught young people the Word of God for 39 years, from 1969 to 2008. I am now 74 years old and I continue to teach the Word of God to both Christians and non-Christians, children, adolescents, young people and adults. I am so amazed now at how God was directing my life even before I knew Him. I am now 100% sure that I have the gift of teaching that God has given me to work in His ministry for His glory.

How did you come to know Christ as your Lord and Saviour?

I heard the gospel around 12 or 13 years of age. One time, I found some pretty, colourful pages at my Aunt's house. My Aunt warned me about the pages saying, "Felipe, these pages talk about the Gospel. Do not touch them because they will make your head hurt." She then took them away from me.

During my 14-16 years, people would offer me an alcoholic drink called "Chicha." When I did not accept what they were offering me, they would make fun of me and ask me if the reason I did not drink was because I was an Evangelical. This happened time and time again. I asked myself, "What does it mean to be an Evangelical? Perhaps the Evangelicals don't drink alcohol," I thought. I was not too concerned, though, about their poking fun at me. I did not even want to drink, as I thought it smelled terrible.

When I was 19, in 1960, my father wanted me to finish primary school. He sent me to a private Christian school about 25 km from our house. It was during this year that I began to become somewhat independent of my father and my house. I lived with another family near the school, and it was at this school that I found out what the gospel was. The teacher was a Christian and my new friends at the school were Christians also. At night there would be Gospel meetings and I would attend them. The family I boarded with was not Christian. I would tell the lady of the house that I wanted to be an evangelical but she would say, "No! Felipe, don't say that. The Evangelicals do not drink or dance like we do. You need to enjoy your youth."

I stopped talking about it but I continued to feel something in my heart calling me to become a Christian. At one of the Gospel meetings,

I remember singing the song from the Hymnbook, "Hymns and Choruses" no. 155 that says, "When the roll is called up yonder, When the roll is called up yonder, I'll be there." When we finished singing, the teacher explained the meaning of the song to us and said God would not call those whose name is not written in the Book of the Lamb. The phrase, "are not written" penetrated my heart. I wanted my name to be written in that Book but I had so many questions. Some of my friends encouraged me to become a Christian and others did not. I waited around 2 months without making a decision.

It was then, in the month of June, that the principal of the school arrived. His name was Mr. Fredrick Smith, from Florida, USA. I had already decided to accept Christ when the principal came to our school. The day he arrived, we had a welcoming party for him and then a meeting afterwards. I told one of my friends that I wanted to receive Jesus as my Saviour that night and so he went and told the missionary. When the meeting was over, we all began to leave the building and my friend reminded me of what I had told him. We returned to the building where the missionary explained the Gospel to me. I prayed, asking Jesus to forgive me of my sins. The missionary prayed for me and he gave me a Bible. He said, "Felipe, read this Book and grow." I continually thank and praise the Lord, remembering that night on June 21, 1960.

Talk to me about your church and a typical service.

I have been blessed to be in the same church for the past 39 years and a leader in that church for more than 25 years.

Many of the typical evangelical churches are like the following:

1. Sunday School: My church has as its only meeting Sunday morning - the Sunday School. A director leads the opening exercises with some choruses. In many of the churches the musical instruments are native, such as the guitar, charango, flute and goat leather drum. Before the group is divided into classes by age, we read a portion of Scripture. After the classes finish, everyone comes together again in the

sanctuary and each class presents what they had learned in their class. The director gives a summary of the number of Bibles, visitors and birthdays that particular week. The leader of the church, deacon or elder, gives the announcements for the coming week and then the Sunday School is finished with the reading of God's Word and a final prayer.

2. Sunday evenings, along with the weekday services, are led by one of the members that has shown gifting in the areas of worship leading and music. There is always the reading of God's Word in each service. There may also be special music by members of the congregation as well as testimonies and public praises to God.

Obviously, each church is distinct in its order of service; but this is how the church that I attended and served in for many years was.

Talk to me about the missionaries that you met in the past and the ones you know now.

During the 39 years that I ministered at the Bible Institute, I had the privilege of knowing 19 missionaries and their wives. Today, I minister alongside others. I give thanks to God for giving me the capability, love and patience to be able to understand and, above all, get along with all the missionaries across the denominations. It is a blessing to be able to minister together for the Glory of the One God. I see that some of the church leaders in my country, Bolivia, have made the missionaries their enemies. They have made it impossible to work together and this makes me ask myself if they even really know God.

What has been their involvement in the local church?

From what I have seen, all of the missionaries became members of the local church that was already established. This is very good, as it identifies them as Christian missionaries and allows them to be able to share their purpose and goals to serve the Lord. It also allows them to learn the culture of the country and also the local ways of worship.

Some of the missionaries, as time went on, became pastors, elders, deacons, counsellors or Sunday School teachers in the churches.

What are some of the cultural errors that foreigners have made in your country?

One error that I have seen is that the foreigners force certain aspects of their culture on the people of the church. For example, the make a rule that the preacher and director of the service must wear a tie when at the front of the church. Another example is to tell the bride and groom that they have to have a wedding cake at their wedding, or that they need to have godparents or a dozen ushers and bridesmaids. The native churches in my country now have these as the norms but it was not always that way. These things can sometimes be an obstacle for some in the churches.

What are some of the areas of conflict that you have noticed in the foreign community?

I see some conflict in the very mission organizations or between mission organizations. I personally notice this among the missions here in Bolivia and I would imagine it is the same all over the world. These conflicts are between missionaries as individuals (interpersonal) and also between organizations that find it hard to work together. It is hard to understand if we say that we serve the same God and that He is sovereign and absolute. We all work for the same cause and goal. These conflicts are stunting the growth of the church and the mission itself. Nothing develops as it should. We are not following the example of the early church (Acts 2:46-47). This makes me sad; but we need to push forward, obeying the commands of God and following the leading of the Holy Spirit. We also need to examine ourselves and how we influence others towards unity.

Where do these conflicts come from?

Basically, I can say that these conflicts come about because of a lack of faith in God and recognition that He is the Lord of the Harvest. There is more dedication to the organization than to the Great Commission. Maybe the greatest error is that more much emphasis is placed on what is taught rather than on what is shown.

What do you think the foreigner's level of understanding is of your culture and context?

I think a foreigner can understand another person's culture up to around 50% based on information they had read or heard. To understand up to 75%, one needs to live in the country amongst the local people, whether in the city or countryside. It is possible that there would still be a lot more to learn.

If there was an aspect of your culture that you would want a foreigner to be aware of before arriving in your country, what would it be? Why is this important to you?

1) If a missionary wants to work in Bolivia, I would want them to be well-informed about our history, culture and languages of Bolivia. They need to be well-aware of the cost of learning language and culture. I would think this is true for any missionary in any country of the world.

2) It is also important for me that a missionary learns to contextualize and apply the messages and Bible studies of the Gospel of the grace of God that he will preach or teach. It is a Gospel of Grace for the salvation of the sinner through faith in God's Son, Jesus Christ. (John 3:16, "For God so loved the world that he gave his only begotten Son, that whosoever believes in Him should not perish but have everlasting life." Vs 36 as well, "He that believeth on the Son, has everlasting life: and he that believeth not the Son, shall not see life; but the wrath of God abideth on him." 1 John 5: 12, "He that hath the Son hath life; and he that hath not the son of God hath not life.")

JUDY – ARAB WORLD

What would you want someone new coming into your area/country to know?

Firstly, study the history of my country carefully. If possible interact with a national and learn its oral history, which has regional variations; e.g., colour, culture, language, and religious sects. The cities are less culturally and religiously

> *I pray that you will come to my country with the Good News that I heard and received, and share the Saviour with my spiritually hungry brothers and sisters.*

conservative than the small towns and villages. In the west of my country it is multi-cultural and a more open society than in the "midlands," which are culturally tribal, and the east which is more sectarian.

Secondly, you will need to understand how gender identity and expectations affect many areas of our lives. Men and women do many things separately in the public sphere. In our restaurants the eating areas are divided between men and families. On the one hand women aren't allowed to drive in my country. But on the other, conversations between the sexes are permitted if dress codes are adhered to; e.g., in public the wearing of the abaya is obligatory for them. We dress well but we understand that Westerners dress more casually. In a society where the extended family is extremely important, expatriate single men and women have to negotiate cultural expectations carefully. Don't be surprised by the efforts made to maintain the expected behavioural norms; e.g., separate male and female waiting rooms in hospitals.

Thirdly, do not make assumptions about the culture. The international media generally labels my culture as unfriendly, but this is inaccurate. "We are very friendly." Never assume stereotypes. This is particularly true of my country. The majority of our population is young and loves change, new ideas and the latest "big thing," especially when it is related to technology. Because of our comparatively recent affluence and fast population growth we could be described as having a "teenage" mentality culture. Language changes fast, too. I have lived outside my country for 10 years and my relatives have described some of the words I use as "outdated."

Fourthly, "during Ramadan don't eat or drink in front of a Muslim." For non-fasting expatriates there may be special areas for consuming food; e.g., hospital canteens.

Always remember that in my country, "Islam is culture more than it is religion."

"Don't bring a Bible into the country, print or electronic. Download a Bible when you arrive."

Learning Arabic is not essential, but it is an advantage. Expatriates with Arabic are appreciated and knowledge of the language will stimulate conversation.

Finally, "Don't be afraid to ask if you don't understand something."

What behaviour or approach would definitely not be a wise thing for a newcomer to demonstrate?

Initiating the sharing of the Gospel directly with one of my countrymen or women can be a punishable offense, usually expulsion; but can be preceded with a period in prison. Live a life that stimulates local people to become inquisitive and ask questions. Answering questions is polite and defending the faith will normally bring respect among my people. There are a lot of misunderstandings about biblical Christianity in my country. For example, they think being Christian is to embrace immorality. Use the Bible, especially the moral expectations of new life in Christ to refute this. Collect all the biblical verses which indicate the demanding morals of being Jesus-shaped people; e.g., lust/adultery, hate/kill (see Sermon on the Mount), and be prepared to explain that the moral behaviour God expects of those who follow Jesus is more demanding than in Islam.

Be respectful of your host country but do not compromise the Gospel. However, do not put yourself into danger. All Westerners are assumed to be "Christian," so live out Christ by your exemplary moral behaviour.

What do you think is the most important thing for a foreigner to understand about your culture/people?

Be prepared to be part of a collective culture. We "share food together" and socialise a lot, especially within our gender groups, but watch out for regional differences.

Though friendly, expect the local community to keep a respectable distance between themselves and you, the expatriate community. So, for example, if one-to-one relationships develop it raises local suspicion. Do things in groups; i.e., several nationals with several expatriates. This makes one-to-one/face-to-face discipleship difficult but can be circumvented through using appropriate secure Internet means. Visible social media should be avoided for these relationships.

The current generation of women works and there are fewer full-time "housewives." For example, "All my sisters and aunts work full-time." Women work predominantly in the health and education sectors but are to be found increasingly in the banking and retail sectors.

We are an "eating out" society, so men and women can be met in coffee shops, restaurants and shopping centres. For a family, the wife can invite local women (in groups) to their home. Gyms are an option but note regional variations; e.g., used more by women than men in my country.

In my country the women are more educated than the local men who engage in past-times such as tafheet (street racing). The result is that more women than men are willing to consider the claims of the Gospel. However, it is still a predominantly male society and the absolute authority is in the local ruler.

How would you like to see new people relate to/partner with your church/other national Christians/expatriate Christians?

In my country the local church is "invisible," so relationships with national Christians have to be handled very wisely. The majority of your public Christian activities will be in officially recognised or tolerated locations. To worship or gather outside these locations is illegal.

Don't be shocked by "modern day slavery" for some Christian expatriates from poor countries who work as house workers/servants. Some may be in abusive situations. If you have home help you can demonstrate a Christian way of employment.

Please respect those who become followers of Jesus in my country by listening to them, learning from them, walking in discipleship with them at their speed. Lay aside your "today" agenda and pray for the Father's. Follow the strictest guidelines of confidentiality. They may face martyrdom for their belief, while you are merely deported.

Please remember to follow the communications security protocols that you will receive.

If you could speak to a group of young workers being trained in the West, going to your country, what would you say to them?

I would say study the society before you go and don't be afraid to talk to people, because they are not as closed as you think. If you want to invite people out occasionally don't be afraid to do this.

Pray with my people and ask the Holy Spirit to speak to them.

At the beginning, "getting the Holy Spirit" is as important for a Muslim seeker from my country as reading the Bible and engaging in apologetics. Once a Muslim is receptive to the Holy Spirit then they will want to read the Bible and apologetics; e.g., the Trinity, the divinity of Christ, the crucifixion, and the inspiration of the Scriptures will be instructive rather than combative.

This may sound strange but be prepared to learn about atheism. Those who leave Islam and turn to Christ often pass through an atheistic phase. They become disillusioned with the concept of "God/Allah" and "religion/deen" and prefer not to believe in an ultimate being. Sometimes people even become "Christian" (religiously) and then adopt atheism and then return to "Christ." The issue of creation is particularly important to study.

I hope that you have found my comments helpful. I pray that you will come to my country with the Good News that I heard and received, and share the Saviour with my spiritually hungry brothers and sisters.

Pray, pray, pray . . .

JETHRO – GHANA

Tell me your story: where you were born, about your family and upbringing etc....

I was born in Enchi in the Western Region of Ghana. I have four other siblings, one girl and three boys. My parents were missionaries. I grew up at

> *Some foreigners make a mistake of thinking that all Africans are beggars and want to receive something from them as foreigners.*

Princess Town in the Ahanta West District of the Western Region. We all lived there for many years because that was where my father was stationed as a missionary.

Where did you go to school?

My pre-school and Primary Education happened at my home town, Enchi. I then attended Junior High School at the Princess Town Roman Catholic Government School, also in the western region of Ghana. After passing Basic Education Certificate Exams, I proceeded to Tarkwa Secondary School and then University of Ghana for my secondary and Tertiary education respectively.

Are you employed and if so what are you doing now?

Yes, I currently serve as a missionary with Pioneers -Africa. My role is that of coordinating Mobilization.

Are you married? How did you meet and marry? Kindly share your story.

Yes, I met my wife while I was facilitating a course at Kwame Nkrumah University of Science and Technology - distance learning centre in Accra. The course was a top up for Polytechnic graduates who wanted to have a first degree. My wife was then one of the class representative and so we got close through that and later on got married as the relationship matured.

How did you meet Jesus? Share you testimony briefly.

I grew up in Christian family, so I was always in and out of Church. We usually have daily devotions. However, I got to personally accept the Lord Jesus Christ at age fourteen when I fell very sick and nearly lost my life, but was miraculously healed after my family fasted for a week for me. My father took the opportunity to explain the need for me to personally accept Jesus and mature in my walk with Him. I gave my life to Christ and got baptised by immersion a few days later.

What sort of church do you attend? – tell about a typical Sunday service

I have attended mostly Pentecostal churches throughout my life. Usually, on a typical Sunday, the service begins with prayer, then hot songs are sang amid drumming and dancing. A first offering is then collected. This is followed by a time of solemn worship and choir then come to minister to prepare the congregants for the preaching of the Word of God. The pastor then preaches and prays for church members. A second offering is collected before announcements are read. There is a special time of prayer at the end by all congregants before the Senior Pastor comes to pronounce blessings upon church members.

Do you have any relationship or connection with the missionaries living in your city/town/area?

Yes

What do you feel about their involvement in the Churches?

I think most of the missionaries are doing their best to help local Churches to advance. They usually help Churches in the area of financial support and run seminars for pastors to equip them to be able to rightly divide the word of truth.

What are some of the common cultural mistakes or misunderstandings foreigners make in your country?

Firstly, I think many foreigners do not take time to learn and understand the basis for many of the traditional beliefs and practices we have in my country but are quick to speak against some of these practices as evil. Secondly, some foreigners make a mistake of thinking that all Africans are beggars and want to receive something from them as foreigners. Also, some of them are not willing to integrate with the community yet they hope to serve them one way or the other.

What are some of the areas of conflict that you observe among the foreign community?

1. Communication gaps
2. Time management issues
3. Community living
4. Clothing choices
5. Manners

Where do you feel these arise from?

In our culture we are more indirect than direct when we want someone to know they are guilty of something. Also, we rely more on verbal agreement rather than written agreement. We live very much as a community and so people can easily visit others in their home without informing them ahead of time. Our way of handling time is also different than what prevails in some countries. Greetings and gestures mean a lot in our country and culture. Our dressing styles may also vary and as such there are some dressing styles that may not be culturally acceptable in some our localities.

How do you feel about their levels of understanding concerning your culture and context?

I think some understand our culture and context because they are willing to learn and adjust their life where necessary. For many others, I would say they feel their culture is better than ours so they care little about understanding it. Some actually look down on our culture.

If there was one aspect of your culture you would like them to know before they came to this country what would that be? (Why is this important for you?)

Our appreciation for greetings and some of our basic manners such as respect for the elderly, not greeting with left hand, etc. I think this is very important because the foreigner will not be accepted in the community if they do things that people perceive as demeaning and insulting to them even if they are ignorant and naive. It can actually run them into trouble.

MARIA – BULGARIA

What do you think a missionary should know about what it is like to come and work here?

Our psyche is greatly influenced by the drama of our historical past

I think a missionary should have an idea beforehand about the country, its government, its people worldview, its culture, its religion and its language.

Would you be a bit more specific?

A missionary should be aware of the country's government and how it functions. The missionaries should be prepared for the difficulties as a result of the cultural differences between the country where they will work and the country they are coming from. Also it's very important to know beforehand the information about the peculiarities of the local language.

What should the missionary know about the Bulgarian's worldview and psyche?

Our psyche is greatly influenced by the drama of our historical past – the long Byzantine and Turkish yoke. The Communists' politics and dictatorship in the past 50 years succeeded to turn our weakened orthodox Christian nation into a nation of atheists and lukewarm Christians. Today's Bulgarians are people open to the world, a bit untrusting and suspicious towards strangers, but always prepared to help in need and a dangerous situation. By nature the Bulgarians are very hospitable people. We are proud that the Bulgarians saved our Jews from the gas chambers of Buchenwald during the years of the Second World War.

What are some of the difficulties in learning the Bulgarian language?
Our language is of the Slavic group of languages; it's not easy to master. It's closest to the Russian language and it uses the Cyrillic – not the Latin - alphabet. I am certain that a good knowledge of the spoken language is most important as a tool of communication for the success in the missionary's work. I speak from personal observations.

What would you like the missionaries to know about the country's traditional religion, about other religions in Bulgaria, and about the religious and historical holidays?
Eastern Orthodoxy is the official religion in our country. It accepts Jesus Christ as God and Saviour, but above all it reveres as a cult the Virgin Mary as "the mother of God"; it venerates the orthodox saints and martyrs. The orthodoxy is full of many religious rituals and traditions. The icons are venerated; the Bible is not studied in the churches. Along with Christmas and Easter there are many other religious holy days associated with the Virgin Mary, the orthodox saints and other pagan holidays revering the souls of the dead, etc.

Our national holiday is 3rd of March – the memorable date connected with the Russian-Turkish war and the end of a five hundred years Turkish yoke. The great holiday we are proud of is "The Holiday of the Alphabet" – 24th of May. We the Bulgarians "gave to all slaves books to read" - a little known historical fact!

Is religion part of the educational system?

No, it's not part of the educational system. "Christian Ethics" is studied only for a few hours in grade 9. It's a pity that Darwin's Theory of Evolution is still studied and not the truth according to the Word of God.

What other religions are popular in the country?

Along with the Orthodox Church in Bulgaria there is a small community of Catholic Christians and many small evangelical Protestant churches. Recently in our capital Sofia was opened a big "Evangelical Christian Centre" with a large Baptist church in it. In Bulgaria 18% of the population are Muslim believers. There are many mosques and many more are being built.

Would you like to share what the attitude and opinion of the indigenous people is toward the evangelical and missionary work in Bulgaria?

In recent years we have seen some spiritual revival. Many small Protestant churches have been planted - Pentecostal, Baptist, Methodist, Congregational, etc. There is hunger and great interest toward the Word of God; thousands of Bibles are given, there are Bible study groups in the evangelical churches. Very useful are the DBS (Discovery Bible Studies), the Old and New Testaments. It's a pity that the evangelization and the missionaries are looked at as a heresy and sects by the indigenous people, thanks to the official opposition and aggression of the Orthodox Church, helped by the local authority and the media at large.

How can the local evangelicals be of help to the missionaries?

For the future missionaries who would work here it definitely will be a little easier, even though the paths are not yet well-travelled and there are difficulties ahead. We are still learning to organize different seminars, preparing future cadre and leaders. At the moment we are involved in Church planting movements (CPM). In the last few years the regional evangelization across Bulgaria resulted in the beginning of CPM. The local evangelical Christians are great help to the missionaries at their arrival, helping them to find living quarters, information about the local authorities, banks, currency, hospitals, teachers in Bulgarian, evangelical churches, police, supermarkets, etc. I would think that it would be good if the sending missionary organization established beforehand local contacts for the help needed.

Would you like to share what are your expectations of the missionaries?

I expect and would hope the local evangelical churches will strengthen, grow and multiply with the help of the missionaries, for God's glory. I expect the missionaries by their lives and giving all to the mission to exhibit God's love and glorify Him. I expect them to demonstrate a spirit of meekness and to be missionaries by conviction, not by convenience.

FREE – CHINA

Interviewer's note:

Brother Free is a young pastor of a church he planted in 2010. He is a mature brother and full of zeal for the Lord, his flock, and the Great Commission. Not only do we share a good relationship on a personal level, more importantly, our church planting team here also has a good working synergy with Brother Free's church on a number of fronts. Not his real name)

> *In order for the locals to be attracted to the Gospel and not your foreignness, try not to talk about how much better your country, culture and people are; but rather, how much we need God, how much we need His forgiveness and grace.*

Brother Free, it's really good to be able to chat with you today and to find out more about your story.

I am happy to be able to do this with you because for us, this kind of conversation is only possible between overseas missionaries and local workers when a good relationship has been first established.

That's great. Can you start of by telling us about your family, upbringing and education?

Ok. Well, I was born and I grew up in a small village in A.H province. I was born in 1981. I will be 35 this year. I was sent by my home church to this city for pioneering mission work back in April

2008. I planted a church among the university students in 2010, which I now pastor.

So that was almost 8 years ago now, when you came. How has it been for you and your family?

It was hard for a few different reasons. Firstly, my wife and I weren't clear ourselves about who to reach out to and even after two years of evangelism, there was no breakthrough.

It was also very hard because I wasn't really interested in pioneering mission work. In fact, I was afraid of mission work because of some bad experiences that other co-workers have had doing mission. It was through a string of events that I ended up in this city, but not really through my own willingness. I did not want to come to this part of China to do mission. Moreover, I heard there are many Muslims in this part of China and I am afraid of Muslims. But God used His Word to give me courage each time I was fearful and finally I submitted to God and to my church. On the 17th of April, 2008, my wife, my little son and I arrived in this city.

But the hardship had only just started. We came to this strange place and had to deal with many adjustments. We came only with some belonging and a map. We didn't know anyone and for the first 3 years, we had no friends. We couldn't even find a place to stay for 3 days. Then on Fridays, we could see throngs of Muslims coming out from the mosque after Friday prayer and we just could not believe we were in China. It felt like we were in a different country. The climate, too, was very dry and our lips would crack and throat uncomfortable, no matter how much water we drank.

The first few years were the hardest, but at the same time, looking back now, it was also the time when I felt I have grown the most in my faith. Even though during those 3 years we had no money, no friends and no pastoral care, God made our calling even more certain for me during those times.

Now my calling and burden is to help our church grow healthily and also to motivate our people to do mission work. I am very certain that the Lord is leading me in this direction.

Praise God! Sounds like now you have a lot of friends, Brother Free. How do you find your overseas co-workers?

Well, I feel that I have really enjoyed interacting with your group of people. Interacting with you guys helps me to consider things from your perspective, as foreigners. It makes me think, if one day the Lord sends some of our people overseas to do some cross-cultural work, how will that look like, what model will work best, etc.?

I also sometimes ponder how we can work together to achieve the best result for our work here, and to be more effective and more efficient. I constantly look for things that I can learn from the missionaries that I know.

You are very kind, Brother Free. Surely we missionaries have brought some kind of inconvenience to the local body. Do you find many of the overseas missionaries cause any unintentional trouble to you guys due to cultural ignorance?

Well, yes, some, but it is not too bad. Every group of missionaries is different from the others, with different team culture and different lifestyle. Out of the missionaries that reside in this region, I can generally put them under 3 categories.

The first group seeks to integrate with the local believers as much as possible and to continually make adjustments with that end in mind. Your group belongs to this category. As you do what you have come here to do, you continually seek to understand us better, how to adapt to the local culture. For example, one of your guys, Brother White and I have had discussions on our cultural discrepancies. These kinds of discussions will help both sides to understand each other's perspective better.

The way I look at it, we are working on the same jigsaw puzzle, but we have the different pieces. Because we have a good relationship, both sides are working together on this same puzzle, putting our pieces to finish this puzzle. I really feel your team has helped us a lot.

For example: Because our Christian history is shorter, in some pastoring and areas of ministry, we lacked good insight or clarity. Your group has helped us in this area, including introducing us to some seminary training. You guys also provide jobs for our people and you encourage us and guide us. The different professional skills and theological knowledge of your team has also been greatly utilized by us for the sake of the work. So we are grateful for this partnership with this group of foreign workers.

Praise God that we have been able to serve you guys this way. How about the other 2 types of missionaries that you have come across?

The second group of missionaries are those who live just in their own circle. It doesn't impact our group very much as there is not much interaction, but I do know that they just live within their own culture. But this group does affect some locals, by "foreignising" them (perhaps even without realizing it). What these foreigners want to impart is the Good News. But some of the locals are also interested in other benefits that come from being associated with foreigners.

What are some of the examples of these benefits of being friends with foreigners?

Like having prestige, employment opportunity and even a chance to go overseas.

I am not closely associated with this group of missionaries, so I am not sure how culturally aware they are about the Chinese people. Perhaps they are not aware, but they do not think of finding out from the locals.

Westerners are usually very direct, meaning they say what they think. But I know our own people are not like that. Chinese people often think one thing, but say a different thing. So I will tell my own people to be careful when interacting with foreigners, including those we are close to, like you guys. If our people are not careful, they might lose the innocence of mutual friendship with foreigners and begin to crave benefits that might come from this friendship.

It is the same with sharing with non-believers. They have heard and watched how wonderful the West is and now that they have a Western friend, they will hope to somehow benefit from this friendship, perhaps even the possibility of going overseas. So they'll do almost anything to be accepted by the foreigners, even if it means having to become a "Christian" and saying the sinner's prayer. Not being truthful is not a problem if being a Christian means they will obtain what they want.

Brother Free, am I right to say that we then need to be careful to separate sharing the Gospel from certain parts of our culture that give the locals the temptation to be associated with us for the wrong motive?

This is a hard one and I don't know if this can be avoided, as in for the locals not to be drawn at all by foreigners and their culture. But there might be things that foreigners can do to minimize this problem. One of them is not by comparing how good your hometown is and how bad the new home is. But going one step further, try to actually like your new home so that when the locals ask, you can honestly say some of the great things about this city. This will minimize the perception that the locals might have, that everything foreign is good.

In order for the locals to be attracted to the Gospel and not your foreignness, try not to talk about how much better your country, culture and people are; but rather, how much we need God, how much we need His forgiveness and grace. We want the locals to think, "Wow, this person's God is so amazing, I want to know Him too!" but not, "Wow, this person's country is so amazing, I want to go there too." So perhaps this is another example of cultural awareness that foreigners need to have in working in the local context.

Is this a problem within the church too?

Not as much. Our guys will joke with each other as in who has more money, but generally they are not materialistic. But our culture is such that the grass is always greener on the other side, so it's not hard to be tempted to look at some other cultures in a more positive light.

So is it better for missionaries to live as simply as possible in a small apartment and not get a car, so locals won't stumble?

I don't think so. It depends on who you are ministering to. Ultimately, missionaries can ask themselves one very important question, "What do the locals immediately see and think when they think of me?" The answer to this question can help the missionaries to know what actually impacts their local friends the most. Is it their faith? Is it their wealth?

Sounds like you have been pondering deeply about these things, Brother Free!

I have actually.

Well, how about the 3rd group of foreign workers. What are they like?

Well, they just do their own thing and they don't get involved with the local church. Not only that, there might even be some frictions between the two groups. They usually do not respect the way decisions are made by the local church or how it does things. Actually, maybe I shouldn't say this, because I believe every missionary that comes to China actually wants to help in one way or another.

That is ok, Brother Free, it is important that we know this. So were you saying that the attitude of the 3rd group of missionaries is that

they have come to do work and they don't need anyone's help, would this be correct?

Yes, but sometimes it goes further than that. In the process of doing their work, they would take away some members of the local church, both the ordinary sheep, the workers and some gifted individuals. I feel this is not a sensible thing to do. I too have come from outside of this city, but I feel we all come here to help and to build up the local body. One day, the Lord might call us and we will leave this place. The local body will be the one continuing the work. Therefore, while we are here, we ought to serve them, to help them to grow and be healthy, for the sake of God's work and because we love Him.

So taking other people's sheep for the sake of your own group is not only disrespectful to the local church, but also undermining the foundation and unity of the Christian body in this place.

Are there many who belong to this 3rd group? Let's say, if you know 10 missionaries in this city, how many of them would belong to these different groups?

Hmm…out of the missionaries I know, I would say 5 belong to the 1st group, 4 to the second group and 1 that belongs to the last group.

Ok. That's good to know. Well Brother Free, I would like to thank you for taking the time to speak to me today. I sincerely hope that through interviews such as this, sending agencies and future missionaries will learn about which approaches are appropriate and helpful in building the work in a different culture and context.

No problem. I'm glad to share this with you.

PASTOR K – KAZAKHSTAN

What should missionaries preparing to come to Kazakhstan know before arriving?

First of all, they need to know where in the world Kazakhstan is located – ha

If they don't have a close relationship with God, they will become weak, tired, and wear out.

ha. They should know a little about Kazakh history. They should know about the country, the differences between the south/north/east/west and how the Kazakhs are different in those regions and their unique elements. For example, in west Kazakhstan they are more staunch/forward. In the north the Kazakhs speak mainly the Russian language. They should study about Kazakh culture and values.

What do the character of the missionaries need to be like? Their character?

First of all, they need to have a firm faith in Christ. Second, they must be patient. Patience is needed because going to another country is like going to another planet – it is totally different than what they are used to. For example, they won't know the language at first. They will be meeting all types of new people and it will be difficult. They have to be like a psychologist. Some people will be friendly to take advantage of them, others they meet will be true seekers of God, others they meet will have hard personalities and you won't be able to talk with them, others will get angry. So it is important to be patient and persevering.

What kind of missionaries do you not need?

If a person is impatient, if the person doesn't have love, we don't need that kind of person. And learning the native language is very good and important. Regardless of what country a person goes to, they need to learn the native language. If you know their language you will be able to understand their culture and where they are coming from.

How should the person relate to the church?

If a church exists in the place the missionary goes, he should work closely with the local church and not try to work alone, separate from the church. It is critical he/she work with the church because they don't know how long they will be able to stay in that country, and if they must suddenly leave, they need to be able and have the new believers/converts connected with a local church. Also, the missionary can be advised by the local church about certain local conditions and situations that he/she otherwise would not be aware of or notice. So he/she needs to work in close consultation with the local church in doing their ministry. They should work with the church's pastor and church's leadership. They should not try and work independently, but in unity with the church.

If you were to go and speak to a group of missionaries about to come to Kazakhstan, what is the most important thing you would tell them?

Regardless if it is missionaries coming, pastors coming, or simply believers coming, the most important thing is their own personal relationship with God. If they have a close relationship with God, then it doesn't matter how difficult a situation is where they find themselves; they will be able to overcome. If they don't have a close relationship with God, they will become weak, tired, and wear out. They won't be able to pray for people. But if they have a firm faith in God, then they won't be afraid of anything, they won't tire out, they won't be overcome. So the most important thing is a person's personal relationship with God.

KEN – GHANA

Tell me your story: where you were born, about your family and upbringing etc....

I was born in Accra the capital town of Ghana. My parents are very strong Christians and made sure we attended church and prayed regularly. I am the

> *People are generally poor in my context but they have their dignity which must be protected. Some foreigners look down too much on us.*

first son. I have 2 siblings, a girl and a boy. My father was a civil servant, my mum was a banker. We lived in our own house in Accra. We, from time to time, had extended family members visit us. Life was nice and easy growing up.

Where did you go to school?

I started school at a very early age, went through a good preschool, basic school and continued to the tertiary level.

Are you employed and if so what are you doing now?

I am a Civil Engineer involved in Building and Road Construction works.

Are you married? Kindly share your story.

We grew up and schooled in different parts of Ghana, met in Church, and joined the same group along the line. Somehow, we started going out on evangelistic trips to some rural parts of the country together. Being a typical city girl, she had a lot of serious cultural shocks and I was available to help her out seeing I had some experience from visiting my father's village with him when I was younger. The Lord graciously worked things out for us and we got married and are happy together.

How did you meet Jesus? Share you testimony briefly.

A Christian brother told me about our Lord Jesus Christ in my Secondary school and followed me up establishing me in the Scripture Union and Church. He taught me about quiet time, Bible study and prayer, and led me to witness to others. Mine has been a great journey because of the mentoring I received from this brother.

What sort of church do you attend? – tell about a typical Sunday service

I attend a Baptist Church. We start service at 9am with praise and worship. We break for a 45 mins Bible studies from 10am and regroup for the sermon, offering and announcements, closing at around 12 30 pm. Our services are mainly in English with interpretations in some of local languages. We are a Bible believing Church.

Do you have any relationship or connection with the missionaries living in your city/town/area?

Yes, many of them are my good friends. They are generally well behaved, ready to learn, humble, and all out for the Lord. Of course there are a few who struggle with our environment, the filth, public transportation system, security, and health care system to name a few. Recently a few friends have complained to me about the wild dogs that some of them keep for their security claiming these dogs do not do not make the missionaries approachable (I believe this is debatable). Others have also complained that some of them are too direct, boastful and show a" know it all" attitude sometimes. It's a learning curve and many are navigating very well.

What do you feel about their involvement in the Churches?

Many of them are very involved in church work which is very good.

What are some of the common cultural mistakes or misunderstandings foreigners make in your country?

Looking down on/talking down to people. People are generally poor in my context but they have their dignity which must be protected. Some foreigners look down too much on us. Please are we all not created in the image and likeness of God?

Making hasty/ not well thought through promises--- A team came to work in my city. We got them a caterer who did a great job taking care of them. When they were leaving, they were full of praise for the caterer and told him they would see how they could support him to set up a restaurant. The caterer took that to be a promise. When one of our leaders here visited the team, they sent this caterer a small gift of a $100 which our leader gave to the caterer. The caterer however insisted that the $100 was too small and that the team had promised to help him set up a restaurant, estimates of which he had given them before they left. He was certain that our leader had taken some of the money and so reported the case to the police. This would not have happened if the team had thought through the best way to help this caterer with us, the local partners, and if they had not made that hasty promise. Please note that a simple statement like "I will see what I can do about this "can be taken as a promise. Better to surprise people that to make hasty and not clearly thought through promises.

Hit and run type of ministry- Many foreigners especially missionaries come, do great things with practically no follow up plan thus leaving many challenges behind them.

Not doing due diligence in checking background of people they want to work with;- Some missionaries come to our part of the world to work with whose background they do not spend time checking then when they are duped or put in trouble they start blaming everybody apart from themselves. Others come over with people who are either not Christians or committed to Christian principles. Many of these tourists just come to give us troubles.

What are some of the areas of conflict that you observe among the foreign community?

Being too individualistic in a collectivistic environment.

Where do you feel these arise from?

Our guess will be the total depravity of man. You know that is the root cause of sin and it is everywhere.

How do you feel about their levels of understanding concerning your culture and context?

Very few invest in learning the culture well. Many see "too many demons" in the culture and so would rather not be a part of that. They think they know but that is a joke. Let me be quick to add that the older ones did far better.

PHILIP AND SALOME – INDIA

What would you want people to know before they come?

One of the first things we would like for newcomers who want to serve here is to understand our culture without being judgmental; they need to be culturally

> *God's work has already been set into motion and when that is undermined, it can be really offensive.*

sensitive. For example, in our communication, unlike several western cultures, we don't always mean what we say. So sometimes a "yes" may actually mean "no" or an "I will try" may mean "no." Another example would be keeping time for a social event. In India we are event-oriented and not time-oriented, so if someone invites us for dinner we do not go exactly on time or leave on time. So, feel free to go late. And if people arrive late at your place, know that they are actually on time. These dynamics are part of our cultural construct, and are not moral issues. So please be non-judgmental and sensitive towards these cultural differences.

Another aspect related to being culturally sensitive would be to know that the Indian culture is a "shame culture." So for example if someone is pregnant, they won't immediately share it, not until the third month, since a miscarriage will cause shame to the family.

And a big one would be that society here is collectivistic. Much of life's meaning is derived from life in community. Hence, issues such as conversion are not purely dependent on the individual's choice. They have serious social implications. The decision to change one's religion is extremely complex and stressful for the person. So be careful not to pressure people of other faiths to convert as soon as they show willingness to follow Christ.

Another aspect related to culture would include respecting our culture and treating people here as equals. We have so often seen this "we are pouring into your lives" kind of posture. Although this attitude may often be tolerated and even "respected" by the Indians, remember that behind such respect you receive (especially the white missionaries) are the values of colonialism etched on the Indian minds ever since the British Raj. Try not to continue these values; first, because it is counter-Gospel, and secondly, because you may be perpetuating the age-old unhealthy stereotype of the western missionaries. Even while presenting the Gospel, although you may have to play a more giving role, make sure you communicate respect.

One of the things that has offended and hurt us in the past is that missionaries have lacked sensitivity to God's work that has already been set in motion here in this land. You see, we have heard sermons that actually undermined God's work in this country, and even the work of the many local ministers who toil tirelessly. We do get offended by this, since we believe that the Gospel came here nearly 2000 years ago! God's work has already been set into motion and when that is undermined, it can be really offensive. Also, do not stir the pot too often by challenging or modifying the Indian Christian traditions thoughtlessly. Remember, we are a collectivistic society. Our spirituality thrives greatly on traditions. So, sensitivity in such situations will be an advantage.

Another important aspect we thought of was having focus on relationships and developing a sense of belonging before sharing the Gospel. Often people belong before they believe. And sometimes they may belong, but never believe. It's a difficult reality, but we live with it. So, do know that your unbelieving Indian friends are not a waste of your time.

We also thought it was important for people to see our lives—our values, our responses, just life generally. We have seen people who have preached great sermons and done powerful seminars but our personal interactions with them have revealed double standards by "I am entitled to be served by you, Indians" type of behaviour that seriously disconnects the message and lifestyle.

Also know that how you use your resources (food, electricity, etc.) and the standard of living you portray (whether in your expenditure, or in the vehicles you use, etc.) may have to be scaled down if you intend to connect with and serve the Indian middle class effectively. Lavish use of resources and lavish lifestyles (in comparison to the people you serve) can either communicate unhealthy consumerism and so disconnect you from a majority of the people, or it may connect you to them for the wrong reasons.

Another thing we've been thinking about is the need to strengthen and mentor Indian leaders rather than always depending on other foreigners, or merely replicating western leaders under the Indian skin (sorry for the cynicism). First, while exposure to other leaders may be helpful and even beneficial in many ways, there is nothing like training local leaders to lead here. Secondly, in developing local leadership, trust them and let them grow with their own leadership style rather than imposing your own style, restricting their style and freedom. Failure in this area has often created a lot of dependency (resources, finances) which was in turn exploited.

We realize that coming to a new land can be shocking; however, we would think that learning to see the good of the culture in the midst of the glaring and uncomfortable differences may make the process smoother for both the missionary and us.

We have also felt at times that our country has been represented unfairly by the westerners. While poverty, dirt, traffic and other annoying things may be obvious realities of our country, there is so much more to us! So please represent us accurately. Look at the things done well! Don't only magnify our weaknesses.

One of the things we found very well done by some of the missionaries was developing two-way friendships. Letting the local believing friends speak into your lives automatically communicates equality and respect. It also paves way for real community. This has been a channel of blessing and healing to us so many, many times!

This is one last thing that we feel is a bit sensitive, but we'll mention it to you. We find that very often Indian staff employed in mission agencies are not paid sufficiently and so they have to depend on other donations, etc., to just make basic ends meet. This leads the staff to serve multiple masters, which is a very unhealthy work ethic. Moreover, it is more difficult to raise funds in India than in some of the western countries, since there are no tax benefits attached to religious donations such as these. Secondly, depending heavily on donations leads to poor accountability with tax payments, etc. Thirdly, insufficient pay scales also create an unhealthy cycle of dependency for the staff to be able to meet their basic needs such as accessing medical facilities, giving a decent education to their children, etc. So if you are employing Indian staff, as much as possible, pay them sufficiently.

Sorry, if we have sounded rude and judgmental. A lot of these comments come from our negative experiences with a few missionaries, and the contrast between these missionaries and the other missionaries who have been good examples. So, pardon us for not being gracious enough. We're still learning. Thank you for giving us this opportunity to share our thoughts.

ELISEO – SPAIN

The first factor is that the missionaries that come should be unable to be content doing anything else. They should be people whom God has captivated with mission and whom he has called to serve here with us and among us; people who couldn't be satisfied doing anything else because God has called them to it.

Without God's calling no one survives in ministry. If they do, they do so according to their own perspective and in their own strength. We want people whom God is driving and guiding. We want people that display the fruit of the spirit and the benefits of that fruit. We want people that are able to embrace us so God may use them to both encourage and discipline us, and to help us in our personal Christian lives too.

We don't just want people to come to do grand evangelistic campaigns, we want people who integrate into the local church and who live their lives together with us, become our dear friends from God and who can care for our hearts and allow us to care for their hearts too.

And after their call, the next most important factor is their heart: People who come with a heart full of respect and humility; with open

> *Theology is great, but all of that theology needs to change their heart and become real so that when they arrive where God has sent them to, the people there will recognise too that God has sent them, and this is evident only through their heart.*

hands to help us. Not people who come with a sense of superiority and pride to try and fulfil mission in Spain independently. They should be people in whom we can see Jesus in their hearts, people who can walk with us in humility, serve, bring God's blessing to us, but also allowing God to bless them through us.

We really want people that integrate, and who walk among us, not over or apart from us by doing their own thing. Instead we want people to integrate into the local church, who love the local church, who love the believers here, who come to bless us and carry us along in mission, and invest in and through the local church.

We believe in the local church, we believe that the local church is the body of Christ, we believe that the local church is a sample of what the universal church of our Lord is like, and we believe that Jesus established his church. So, for us the church is something that is very important. The church is something that is continually growing and developing.

We're not closed to those things which support the local church and help the local church fulfil the things that the local church should be doing, like a Bible seminary for example. We believe in the call of God on people to prepare themselves in those institutions, but Jesus came to establish the church. For that reason the local church is the heart of every other ministry expression.

If someone is not able to join the local church, respect the local church, work with the local church; that is like signing a cheque for disaster here in Spain. It's like placing an expiry date on all that you're doing. Sooner or later it will expire and it will disappear, but the church will continue to be because it is from God. For that reason it is so important that the people who come are not just attending the local church, but also integrated into the local church by giving of their hearts, their lives and their gifts.

In Spain, missionaries are considered to be in one of two categories. The first is those whom we regard as a gift from God - a blessing. Someone who comes to help, to contribute, and walk alongside and who comes to help you even in your own spiritual life. And then on the other hand there are many Spanish church leaders who, due to a negative missionary experience, don't want anything to do with them. This is generated by those whose attitude is that of: "We have come to teach you how you need to do things here." And this is something that has done a lot of damage to the mission in Spain. As a result many churches are closed to receiving or working with missionaries more than at a superficial level.

The best way for missionaries to work and communicate vision is from within, as opposed to bringing critique from the outside. The first thing they should do is to join the local church and become part of the church so that the church senses that the missionary loves them. This is then reciprocated by the church and the missionary can speak from this position of being part of, one with, and from within the church. It's from this posture that the missionary can, with much prayer and love, and through the leadership, highlight needs that are not being met and how he believes those needs should be met.

God's work is God's work, and so we have to believe that God will move our hearts. The solution is never to do something parallel or apart from the leadership of the local church. That is never the solution. The solution is always to do it from within with love, speaking to the hearts of the people on God's behalf, and waiting for God to do the work.

Integration into the church and into the culture is key. The missionary has to root themselves in Asturian families. Just as anyone else in the church, they would have different levels of friendship and the missionary has to be active in this and inviting people in the church to eat with them and pass time with them learning about what we think, who we are, our expressions, and little by little becoming part of the culture.

Because these people are outside of their context, it's important that they too have relationships that help and support them emotionally and spiritually inside the local church. This is something that God will do whenever the missionary and the church are open to it and care for one another. It is a natural form of seeing who we are, otherwise they'll go from home to church to home again, and they will meet with other people of their culture and they'll never be able to integrate more into the culture and understand how we feel.

I appreciate it's very difficult. The Asturian is cold and hard at the beginning and he finds it hard to give himself to others. If a missionary goes to Andalusia, they'll have 100 friends in no time. But when they come to Asturias it will take them time to find just 1 friend. In that aspect, we are more reserved and cold at the beginning; but when we do form friendships we give ourselves completely, we are passionate in sharing our homes and our lives.

In the north, the missionary will be rejected just because he is a missionary. He will find himself among people who are slow in opening themselves to him, but once they are open he will have them in his hands. Asturians are very faithful, and when they do give themselves, they give themselves completely. The Asturian is proud of his roots, his land, and his beliefs.

Religion isn't as deep or present in the Asturian as in those from the south of Spain, though there are religious people. This region was severely punished in the dictatorship (Editor's note: the fascist dictatorship of Francisco Franco was from 1939-1975) and by the Catholic Church and so people are very reserved when it comes to anything that is associated with the word "religion". This is a very tough area for the gospel. So it will be difficult to have conversations with people about the Bible because in the north, because the majority don't want anything to do with Jesus.

So, Spain is a hard country toward the gospel. That's why the missionaries who come are a blessing because they contribute freshness, vision, and another way of doing things, presenting the gospel and living the Christian life, which is always enriching. But I would say that, in general, Spain is a very hard place for the gospel.

God's people in Spain need people who live their Christian lives naturally and with freshness. Because the evangelical movement has suffered much under the dictatorship and through certain church traditions this has caused many people to view the Christian life as living a series of rules rather than a daily walk with God.

We also need people who contribute a wider vision, different ways of ministering to people, of contributing ideas about forming Bible study groups or spiritual growth which in one way or another could attract people. Right now the people in Gijon are reticent to sit down and read the Bible. They may not have a Bible or if they do they have never opened it. They are the two great areas of contribution that missionaries can have in this area.

If I were to speak to a group of missionaries at the point of coming, I would say that there are many great theological books in their language which they should bring and read in their homes, but that there are no books that tell you the heart that you have to have, and this is something that God has to do in each person's heart. And when God captivates their hearts for mission and they obey the calling and come, they need to maintain their hearts in a posture of simplicity and humility before God, so that it is always God and not oneself. Because when it is God, the heart of the missionary is a special heart and one that I have seen. When someone sees that heart they give thanks to God and open their arms to it. When they see a lot of theology and achievements, there will always be suspicion and fear to move forward. But when someone sees the heart that kneels before God, that loves, that wants to serve and help, we become those who kneel to receive the blessing from God. So I would say to them that they need to care for their heart. Theology is great, but all of that theology needs to change their heart and become real so that when they arrive where God has sent them to, the people there will recognise too that God has sent them, and this is evident only through their heart.

The perfect missionary in my opinion would be someone who is mature in the Lord. It wouldn't be someone who is new to the faith or recently converted or who is guided by any exaggerated emotions so that when those emotions disappear there isn't anything left. They would have firm Biblical principles that are well established. A person that would have a well-established personal relationship with Jesus. Not a person that needs to be a missionary to initiate a personal relationship with Jesus but a person who already has that well established and a person that is willing to deny himself in many moments. For some people the cultural differences are highly accentuated and it can be difficult and so it would be a person that, for the love of God and the people here, could walk under the direction of local elders or a local pastor within the margins of Biblical principles. People who are humble and know how to listen and learn, not people who are very closed theologically because that would just cause friction in the church. That they know how to listen and understand and whose life reflects someone's life who loves God.

With regard to gifting, we're sure God will reveal the gifting of that person and that they would execute those both within and outside the church, but first come in the heart that this person has and the attitude toward the work, the local church.

The profile of someone that we wouldn't want to work with would be a person who is very closed, who always has to maintain their way in things, who isn't able to laugh and cry in the church, who is able to teach from the pulpit a distinct line from which the church is heading which would just create divisions, problems, tensions, who thinks more about themselves than in those next to him. I could never work with someone like that, although because of who I am I would try but I think that I would end up throwing in the towel.

Sometimes the church would be prepared to provide a legal covering, but at the point of joining to the degree to which a missionary should join a local church, which is a person who should be equal to any other member of the church and joined to the very life of the church. And this means that there is a barrier for many churches in Spain. And this creates fear that the missionary could arrive with charisma and ability to connect with people and split the church. And to protect against that it creates a great distance to prevent it from happening in the church. And so one might maintain them at a distance, not allow them to enter or join.

In this dependency in prayer and the love shown to the local church they have to share what they think and see and how God is moving them and how they can bless the local church by meeting certain needs, but always from within the church. Not from outside by arriving and saying this is bad or not done that way because that will be perceived as an attack because the person doesn't know, or belong to, or love the church, or the church love them and so it will be perceived as an attack and cause problems.

When a missionary forms part of a church and the church recognises the need and they move to meet the need,

It depends on the church, the gifts that the church has and the resources that the church has. A bigger church with more gifts and resources would have it a little easier with more hands to put to the work. The smaller churches would require the missionary to occupy more roles to be able to carry the work forward. The missionary shouldn't be fearful. He has to be respectful and subject to the elders/pastors but needs to take steps forward without fear.

If a household opens up in a town, perhaps the missionary might have the time to go and work there. But maybe the church has people that could do that too. I believe that the m should function as any other member of that team because he will be part of the team and how it works and he will form part of the discussions with the leadership of how to do thesis things and he has to express his opinion with humility and love and listen to the opinions of others too and work through things openly. He should behave as someone who is a gift from God in the local church and from this point of love and respect can openly suggest what he thinks, and how to do things just as alone else in the church. The m who comes in that way, fulfils this profile, forms part of the church giving example and testimony to everyone showing Jesus in his life this person should be heard in the leadership in the church.

When a missionary enters a new context they do create a certain expectation, and expectations attract. If this person is going to be part of something that lasts there should also be people from the city or nationals so that there is never a sense in which it is perceived to be something for or of the foreigners. So it's always good that it's not just something of the missionary but that there are local people involved in that work and, with all of them, they could do the work together.

KODJO – TOGO

Tell me your story: where you come from, your family and your education.

I was born in a polygamous family. My dad had four (04) women. The village of my birth is called Yéviepé in the prefecture of Kloto, Togo. I did my Primary and Junior High school Education in Badou, Wawa Prefecture; Senior High School in Ghana in the

> *The expatriate is called to understand that life is an appointment to give and receive; and that in his encounter with a welcoming culture, he will have as much to learn (to receive) as to give.*

aftermath of the 1990-1993 political crisis. After my Bac A2 in 1994, I obtained a degree in Theology in 1998 in Lome, Togo, then a Master in Missiology in 2014.

Are you employed and what do you do now?

I am a Missionary with Pioneers-Togo, serving as Administrator and Training Coordinator.

Are you married? Please share your story.

I am married. My wife's name is Christine and we have the grace to have 3 children. My wife and I are known in our church, Christine was very dedicated and served as a singer and pianist. I serve as youth and student pastor. We engaged in 2000 and were married June 21, 2001 in Lome.

Do you have a relationship or link with the many foreign and foreign NGOs that came to work in your country?

Yes

What do you think of these different groups?

They have a significant role to play in these countries

What are the traditional belief systems of your culture and how do you feel about them?

Hospitality ... These different groups are welcome in the country; to help the poor, bring their knowledge to development.

What do you think of Christian churches in this country?

Churches are places where we worship God. They pray that God will bless people and the land, that God will give rain ... and eternal life.

How did you meet Jesus? Briefly share your testimony.

I was courting a girl who was a member of the Church of the Assemblies of God of our neighbourhood in Badou. One of those Saturday nights when I met her, during the holidays in 1989, she told me that if I agreed to come to church the next day, she would become my girlfriend. This is how I went to the church the next day to seduce her. But during the preaching, the Holy Spirit touched me by showing me my sinful situation and the condemnation that weighed on me. At the call of the pastor, I got up to give my life to Christ confessing my sins and asking for forgiveness. I then became a new creature.

What kind of church do you frequent? - Tell a typical Sunday service

I attend an Evangelical Pentecostal church. Sunday worship begins with a time of prayer, followed by songs of praise, Bible studies, offering, preaching and prayer, announcements and final blessing.

Do you have a relationship or connection with missionaries living in your city/town?

Yes, I have often participated in programs with expatriate missionaries; we also sometimes worked together.

What do you feel about their involvement in the Churches?

It often depends on their orientation and purpose for which they came. Those who have come to work with national churches are easily involved in the activities of said churches to achieve their goals. Those who have come to establish their own church are also working within this vision. Whatever their purpose, they contribute directly or indirectly to the life of the church in general.

What are some of the common cultural mistakes or misunderstandings foreigners make in your country?

Often expatriates are considered demi-gods, perfect people who know everything and have the answer to any problem ... before folks realize soon enough that they are men and women with limits and gaps as well, and therefore need local the local folks as much as they need them.

What are some of the areas of conflict that you observe in the foreign community?

Areas of conflict within the expatriate community can be observed in their approach to ministry practice (mission) in the field. It is easy to see that, despite their good will and their considerable financial and material resources, they often struggle to obtain results.

Where do you feel these arise from?

This, in my humble opinion, is a misunderstanding of the expatriate's role in the success of a project, program, or mission in a host country. The expatriate needs to recognize his role of trainer, mobilizer, and coach, and support the locals to reach their own people.

The expatriate is called to understand that life is an appointment to give and receive; and that in his encounter with a welcoming culture, he will have as much to learn (to receive) as to give. It would take a good dose of humility and vulnerability to value the contribution of the local team while bringing his touch from the outside.

What do you feel of their levels of understanding concerning your culture and context?

Expats often have a globalized understanding of other peoples, imbued with a superiority complex.

If there was one aspect of your culture you would like them to know before they came to this country what would that be? (Why is this important for you?)

The deep understanding of equality between all races and peoples is a liberating necessity; because cultures and traditions, though they may seem strange to those who do not understand them, contain fundamental values that define peoples.

God is the author of creation. In determining the boundaries and abode of every people on earth, He has buried enormous cultural riches that any wise visitor must seek to apprehend at their proper value to better serve this people. To do this, any expatriate who wants to serve among a people, a culture, that is not his own must depart from any consideration of superiority, be quick to learn and discover day by day the said culture; and above all be surrounded by a team maintained on the basis of trust and mutual sharing without bias.

MARIANA – BULGARIA

What do you think is the most important thing for a missionary to know about Bulgaria?

A missionary should know the geographical location of Bulgaria, but above all to know the country's history to be able to understand better the culture of the country and the peculiarities of people's psyche.

> It's necessary to spend a long time and have patience to develop friendship and personal contacts.

Would you be a bit more specific?

For five hundred years Turkish Islam was a big challenge not only for the physical survival of the nation, but also for the conservation of the Christian faith. There has been Islamisation by force. Today 5% of the population are Bulgarians forced to abandon their Christian faith and to accept Islam, the so-called Mohammedans. In 1863 was planted the first Protestant church. The missionaries were first to inform the world about the atrocities of Islam against the indigenous Bulgarians, and this brought about diplomatic intervention by Russia and the West. The Communist dictatorship began a fierce war against the existing Orthodox and Protestant pastors who did not cooperate with the regime. Many of them were sent to prison and camps and many were killed. This persecution continued for almost 50 years, during which time were forbidden the Bibles and any Christian literature.

Today Bulgaria is a member of the European Union. Should this be a concern for the missionary?

Bulgaria's membership in the EU is not a threat for the Christian missionaries. The country needs missionaries because during the Communist regime three generations were deprived of the true Christian faith. Today's tolerant policy of so-called democracy poisons the spiritual climate with a nominal and pagan-ridden Orthodox Christian religion as well with the many sects which it tolerates.

Would you tell me something about the Bulgarian world view and psyche?

The Bulgarian is hospitable and has a good sense of humor, but at the same time is not very trusting of strangers. Because of this, street evangelization and giving tracts do not always bring good results; on the contrary, sometimes people's attitude is negative. It's necessary to spend a long time and have patience to develop friendship and personal contacts.

What are the difficulties in the Bulgarian language?

The Bulgarian language is not easy. From my experience only after a few years the missionaries can express themselves and be understood when they evangelise. That is why it's necessary for them to engage in contacts with the indigenous besides the lessons in Bulgarian.

What would you share with the missionaries about the country's traditional religion?

The Eastern Orthodox Church has become a comingling of Christian traditions without a context – child's baptism and communion for forgiveness of sins. Many are the things from pagan practices, which have nothing to do with Christianity and the Bible. There are religious holidays revering different saints and martyrs daily. Sacrifices for health are often made. The Virgin Mary – "the mother of God" - is revered even more than Christ.

Is religion part of the educational system?

It is not a part of the educational system and I hope it will not become one because the Bible has no authority for the Orthodox Church. Following this logic, the children will not get biblical education; on the contrary they will be taught the pagan rituals, practices and idol worship.

What other religions are popular in the country?

Apart from the Orthodox churches there are Evangelical and Catholic churches and about 18 % of the population are Muslims, There are registered sects: Adventists, Jehovah Witnesses, Mormons, New age, Yoga, the pantheistic teaching "White Brethren," Masons, Rotary Clubs and others.

Can the missionaries count on cooperation from the indigenous Christians?

The missionaries can count on help and cooperation only from the evangelical Christians.

Would you share what is your expectation of the missionaries?

The missionaries must live permanently where they work so that they can witness with their way of life and people can trust them more. The missionary should be able: to speak well the spoken language; to be sincere and friendly; and this should be obvious, not to expect fast results; to be able to communicate well with different age groups; to consult the indigenous evangelical Christians about matters of language and cultural differences; and it's desirable to have musical ability.

NADIA – MOROCCO.

Interviewer's note:

Nadia is bubbly and passionate, with a faith that has been forged by challenges and difficulties she had gone through. She seems at once both strong in and clutching at what she believes is what really matters: her

> *One strategy may work in one group but totally misfires in another. Just because someone has just woken up does not necessarily mean he needs coffee.*

faith in her Saviour. She has been a believer for several years and is still the only one in her family. Right now, she is not in regular fellowship with anyone in her city. This seems to be the case with everyone there, following a series of expulsions in 2010.

Nadia is close to a former worker who served in another city, working with handicapped children. She has also worked with a few associations working among children. Her vision is to establish her own.

I am a very open person. Like a child, I am very spontaneous. I speak what's in my heart. Over the years, life has taught me many things about people and about relationships. I have gone through a lot, been hurt many times; yet, I have remained open and trusting. That is because I have chosen life, and my faith in God has kept me going.

Many people come to Morocco for a variety of reasons. Some because they like the country and her culture. Others because they have the means and the opportunity to come here. Still others because they like it here and they think that everything is nice. These are all very human responses and are understandable.

The same can be said for workers. They come here with the intention to do their job well. However, what they do and what they should do are two different things. In fact, the majority of them do not really work; they just think they do. Let me rephrase that: It is not that they do not work at all; but, that they just "touch." That is, they just scratch the surface of things. They do not go deep enough and far enough.

For workers to succeed here, they should know the culture. This is crucial. Since they are foreigners, this culture will be very different from their own. Family life, language and how it is used to communicate thoughts and feeling, the way people dress, their way of life, how the system works and the like, can be a huge challenge. As such, they must make the time and expend efforts to study the culture, learn it, live with it, and thrive in it.

It is likewise essential that they have eyes to see the people and their needs. They must endeavour to find out what resonates with people, what their dreams and aspirations are, what works with them. Not one size fits all. One strategy may work in one group but totally misfires in another. Just because someone has just woken up does not necessarily mean he needs coffee. He might just be in need of someone to talk to.

Strive to see people. Try to know them. Sensitivity to subjects that will rob them of their own spontaneity towards locals will go a long way. For instance, they must have heard comments like, "Moroccans want benefits, money from foreigners." Then they talk about it among themselves. Consequently, they become guarded in their attitude towards Moroccans. As a result, spontaneity and honesty are lost.

In addition, it is imperative for the worker to build people's confidence in them, that they earn the latter's trust. For instance, I work in the reservation section. For customers to be convinced to part with their money, they must have confidence in me. I need to work on gaining that. When workers have the confidence of people they are working among, the latter feel comfortable, at ease. When they do not, they are bound to lie to the people to gain it. Likewise, people are likely to think that the workers are just lying to them.

Moreover, this confidence-building comes with a heart that listens. Many times, people come to church with concerns, but the workers shut them up indirectly. They either say, "Trust in God" or change the subject completely. People are not stupid; they can feel that. Consequently, people pray with them, work with them; but they are true neither to the workers nor to themselves nor to anyone.

Furthermore, it is important that they be prepared to act as spiritual fathers and mothers. Often, a local Christian is the only one in his family who believes in Christ. Sometimes, he becomes isolated, even in danger. He needs to know that there is a "family" he can go to when things go tough. Otherwise, "Where will I go when I am being attacked left and right, and you don't care?"

As for partnership with the church, let me say that faith is life lived out. Hence, workers should not just talk; they should act. And when they do talk, they should likewise cast the church a vision.

There are many ways by which this can happen. First, realize that it is not important that they remain in one place. They can start a project, supervise it until it gets established, and then move on to another place.

Second, network with the local church. Workers are not going to be here forever. When they go, their project goes. Let it not be. Teach the church how to live and give them skills to do that.

Third, there are many who need help and it is not possible to help all of them. Focus on those that you can. Some of them have a vision to do something and they need concrete, practical help. Help them realize their vision. They cannot work alone, especially since they are no longer Muslims. They are now believers in an environment that can be hostile to them because of their faith.

Lastly, the church does not need more protocols. They need to know how to work together. When people around them see it, they take notice.

Let me close with these words: If workers want to live in Morocco for a long time, they have to be practical. They have to show their faith by their action. They must ask themselves: "Am I ready to help? Am I willing to love, not just in words, but also with action?"

NII – GHANA

What would you want someone new coming into your area to know?

That they are not bringing God to us. We know there is God almighty, we have been worshipping Him in various ways. He has been and will continue to be with us. We depend on Him for everything. We love and respect our culture. Like every culture on earth, we have our challenges. Coming here to tell us our culture is demonic is not only insulting

> *Coming here to tell us our culture is demonic is not only insulting to us, it shows you feel superior to us; you think you have the best and we the rest, and we would not take that in any way. We are very proud of who this God has made us.*

to us, it shows you feel superior to us; you think you have the best and we the rest, and we would not take that in any way. We are very proud of who this God has made us. We know we are also His image bearers just as you are. We also have a lot to offer even though we may be poor and not as formally educated as you are. Come ready to learn from and of us as we also learn from and of you. Let us serve one another that way.

If a missionary was going to come to your town, what would you want them to know before they came?

We love people, for us relationship is paramount and over everything. Our ways may not be their ways but we also have a reason for doing the things we do. If they come ready to learn and understand

and not just that we must by all means understand them and their ways, they would enjoy us as we enjoy them and God will be glorified.

We know they can never become like us just as we can also never become like them. God created us different and it is important we all recognize and respect that and treat one another with respect.

In fact, as far as I am concerned, if a missionary comes to us with an open heart and in a learning posture—as a number of them are doing—(You can see from the results they are getting.) that missionary is sure to achieve great results .

We believe in the spirit world. We understand that the spirit world is alive and active. If a missionary should come to us with very little or no understanding of the spirit world, he/she is bound to become a disaster.

What do you think is the most important thing for a foreigner to understand about your culture/people?

We love God almighty and want to worship Him aright. Our people are very religious. Many of them feel that it is improper to go to God directly, they need a mediator, and for many of them these are the gods. Remember, our culture understands and uses mediators everywhere, being direct can be seen as wrong in many cases. Wow! What a great opportunity to present Jesus Christ as the great mediator without condemning the gods. Condemning our gods have been used by many foreigners and missionaries for years without results because it just does not go down well with our people. I am not sure why some foreigners and missionaries still go that way. Just present Jesus as the great mediator and leave it there and see what results you will get.

Some foreigners talk too much. They ask you a question and whilst you are thinking about the answer many more questions come and get you confused, sometimes before you finish what you have to say they just jump in with more talk. I know our system of education can be blamed for this but who brought that education to us in the first place!?!

How would you like to see new people relate to/partner with your church?

Mutual respect and love—that is the way to go. No signs of racism, superiority complex, etc. And mind you, the foreigner may not be aware, but we smell all these from far. We are able to quickly tell the genuine ones from the mercenaries (Please pardon my strong language here). Let's be careful that partnership is based on our mutually agreed terms and conditions, that may be difficult to get to but not impossible. You see many of my people already feel inferior to foreigners and so must be deliberately drawn in.

If you could speak to a group of young missionaries being trained in the West, what would you say to them?

You may have the resources to serve the Lord very well in every foreign culture but please be sure to enter into the culture with an open heart and as a learner—a lifelong learner—and it will be well with you.

JOIN THE CONVERSATION

We hope you enjoyed your time under the trees, listening to the voices of our friends and family around the world. We are all too aware that this is just a smattering of voices and there are many valuable voices not contained in this small volume.

We hope this brief experience will inspire you to become a lifelong learner. We hope you will seek to listen and will humbly learn from those God brings across your path.

We would like to ask you to consider three questions:

1- How have you benefited from this book? What are the lessons you are taking with you from our global family? Don't let the learning stop here. Keep listening.

2- Who do you know who would profit by reading this book? Please tell them about it or better yet, buy them a copy. Don't let the conversation stop here. Start more!

3- Would you consider adding your voice to the conversation? Or perhaps you would like to interview someone? We are eager to continue the conversation and are open to receiving additional submissions! We promise to read every single submission. If we get enough, we would love to publish another volume of voices, as we carry on this family discussion. Please send your voices to voices@peregrinipress.com. We look forward to continuing the conversation.

BOOKS FROM PEREGRINI PRESS

All hard copy editions are available wherever fine books are sold. All titles are also available as Kindle e-books to read on whatever digital device you prefer.

The Field Notes Series
  Forged on the Field
  Voices from the Field

The Our Stories Series
  Pursuit of a Thirsty Fool: 5 Years Down the Road and Still Thirsty
    ~by T.J. MacLeslie
  Far from Cold ~by Gillian Newham
  Blue is the Color (Coming Soon) ~by Anne Childs

Also by T.J. MacLeslie
  Designed for Relationship – 5th Anniversary Edition (Coming Soon)
  The Advent of Relationship

Connect with us:
  Email: info@peregrinipress.com
  Web: www.peregrinipress.com
  Twitter: @peregrini_press
  Instagram: peregrini_press
  Facebook: https://www.facebook.com/peregrinipress/

Made in the USA
Coppell, TX
01 September 2021

61637053R00094